DIY
INDUSTRIAL PIPE
FURNITURE & DECOR

Creative Projects for Every Room of Your Home

JAMES ANGUS

Ulysses Press

For my mother, Sheryl.

"Look, Mom, I wrote a book."

Published in the United States by
Ulysses Press
P.O. Box 3440
Berkeley, CA 94703
www.ulyssespress.com

ISBN: 978-1-61243-606-7
Library of Congress Control Number: 2016934489

Printed in the United States by Bang Printing

10 9 8 7 6 5 4 3 2 1

Acquisitions Editor: Casie Vogel
Managing Editor: Claire Chun
Editor: Renee Rutledge
Proofreader: Kate St. Clair
Front cover design: Michelle Thompson
Interior design: what!design @ whatweb.com
Layout: Jake Flaherty

Distributed by Publishers Group West

CONTENTS

INTRODUCTION

I have never been one of those people who would let a lack of funds stop them from getting the look they want. In my line of work, retail creative services, I have to be extremely resourceful. There's just no other way. Because I have to create manor house interiors in store windows for only a few hundred dollars, I've learned to paint faux limestone, "sew" pillows with a stapler, and electrify vintage light fixtures. ("Vintage" usually means they came from a trash heap in front of an old house.) Nothing is ever thrown away. Everything can always be spray painted, retrofitted, or reconstructed to fit some future installation. I definitely take that philosophy home with me.

Every apartment and house I have lived in over the past 20 years has been left much improved for the next inhabitant. I do so much more than simply paint the walls, trim, and ceilings. (Always paint your ceilings a fresh white. It makes the biggest difference—trust me.) I've removed nasty carpeting and refinished the hardwood floors underneath, installed my own recessed lighting, laid tile floors, hung new ceiling fans, brushed chrome switch plate covers, and even lined an entire set of kitchen drawers with cork. In my last place, half of a 1930s Tudor cottage on the famed Dallas M streets, my brother and I replaced the cheap big box–store bathroom sink with a higher end vintage pedestal sink (rescued from another junk pile), and my partner Jamie and I dismantled the dilapidated screened-in porch and rebuilt it from the ground up. I even made shutters and window boxes from cedar scraps for all the windows. On a rental.

Then I *bought* my first house. (Cue the sound of angels trumpeting.) Now there really were no limits.

In just six years, I've torn down walls, covered over unnecessary doors, refloored, completely replaced the electrical panel and every light fixture, constructed a wood accent wall, updated a very outdated kitchen, clad the garage interior with cedar planks, hung factory-style pendants, built a horizontal slat fence and a 300-square-foot deck, installed lights under the eaves, re-landscaped, and (hopefully, by the time this book is published) completely gutted and remodeled the master bathroom.

Did I say there were no limits? Because there is always that one limitation: money. Most everything I've done has been on a shoestring budget.

"So how does all that lead to plumbing pipe?"

I knew you'd ask.

About 15 years ago, at one of my favorite pizza joints, I noticed that the logs for the wood-burning oven were contained with industrial pipe "towers" attached to the walls. I was immediately smitten and wanted to try the same thing in my rental, even though I didn't have a working fireplace—or even the empty wall space. But I never stopped thinking about it. My current house has a working fireplace and room for wood storage. A little online research led me to a rolling log holder at a fancy decor store that I could never afford, and a light turned on in my head. I combined those two inspirations in my garage and a day later, had a rolling log holder made from humble industrial plumbing pipe and scrap 2 x 4s. It was a fraction of the cost of the mail-order piece, movable, and relatively easy to make. I posted a few pictures online, with some basic directions, and it took off like wildfire. Not only were people making their own versions (I know because they sent me pictures of their finished projects), they were also asking if I would make them to sell. As if I had the free time.

From there I was constantly on the lookout for new ways to use plumbing pipe. We needed curtain rods. Why not use pipe, with drop cloth curtains? Everyone online was making shelving units from pipes. How could I make mine look different? If something made from steel caught my fancy, I duplicated it with pipes.

In fact, there isn't a room in our house that doesn't have industrial pipe in it in some way.

And now, with this book, I'm passing my projects on to you fine readers. But, please, don't let my humble directions stop you from experimenting on your own.

Make yours unique.

Make it fit your needs.

Make it with industrial pipe.

WORKING WITH INDUSTRIAL PIPES

Standing at the hardware store looking at a wall of pipes and pipe pieces, you will find yourself wondering, "How do I begin?" It can be a little intimidating but don't fear. I'm here to explain it all to you.

GETTING TO KNOW YOUR PIPES

Most of the pipe you'll find in hardware stores is made of carbon steel. Galvanized silver pipe, traditionally used just for water transport, is coated in zinc to make it more corrosion resistant. Black pipes are used for transporting gas and oil, but not water, because they rust easily. This is a good thing to know if you plan to use your finished pipe pieces outside. Silver is better. Unfortunately, because of the zinc coating, silver pipes tend to be a little more expensive.

Most new plumbing builds are done with PVC pipe.

MEASURING PIPE AND FITTINGS

You will notice that plumbing pipe and the corresponding fittings come in an array of sizes; anywhere from ⅛-inch up to 5 feet in diameter. (It's important to know that diameter refers to the inside distance of the pipe opening. This is a good thing to remember when you're drilling a hole in a board for a pipe. For example; a ¾-inch-diameter pipe will need a hole just slightly larger than 1-inch to fit through.) Your standard neighborhood hardware store will probably only stock an assortment of 4 to 5 of these sizes. The most commonly used pipe diameters are: ⅜-inch, ½-inch, ¾-inch, and 1-inch.

Length refers to just that; the length of the pipes and nipples. Most hardware stores will offer a variety of nipples from 1 inch up to 12 inches in length, and pipes up to 8 feet long. Can't find the length you need? Just ask someone to cut it for you.

In this book, most projects will use the same diameter pipes and corresponding fittings for all of its supplies. Each project will tell you what kind of diameter to buy. For example, "Use ½-inch-diameter black pipes and fitting." For the more complicated projects that require pipes and fittings with different diameters, diameter will always be listed first and then followed by length. For example, a project might ask for a "½ x 18-inch pipe." The ½ measurement is diameter and the 18-inch measurement is length.

IDENTIFYING FITTINGS

Pipe fittings, galvanized and black, are all made of malleable iron.

There are a couple dozen different fittings, each with a specific purpose, but we'll be focusing on the fittings that are readily available at your local hardware store for the projects in this book. (Can't find that one specific piece at your store? I guarantee that you can find it online. Check the resources in the back of this book.)

Elbow: An elbow is exactly what it sounds like it would be, a pipe connector with a bend in it. Like a human elbow. Usually the bends are 90 or 45 degrees, but it's not unusual to find others. If the ends are different sizes, meant to restrict water flow, it's called a reducer elbow.

Street Elbow: Like an elbow, a street elbow creates a bend in between two pipes. But street elbows have one male end and one female end.

T: The most common pipe fitting, a T has one inlet and two outlets. One of the outlets is usually at a 90-degree angle from the other two. The outlets can be larger or smaller than the inlet. If so, this is called a reducer T.

Cross: Similar to a T, but with one inlet and three outlets. Crosses are not very commonly used in plumbing because of the stress they put on pipes, but they have become popular lately because pipe enthusiasts have started crafting with them.

Union: A union simply joins two pipes of the same size together.

Reducer Union: A reducer is a fitting used to connect two different-sized pipes together. With water flow, it reduces the amount of water getting through the pipe. Regardless of which end is the intake, this piece is never referred to as an expander.

Nipple: A nipple is a short piece of pipe used to connect two other pieces of pipe together, female end to female end. A close nipple will have no unthreaded area and can only be removed by twisting apart the pieces it connects, or with a nipple wrench, which grips the inside of the pipe so as not to damage the threads.

Flange: A flange is used to attach a toilet, or water closet, to a drain pipe. It sits flush with the floor.

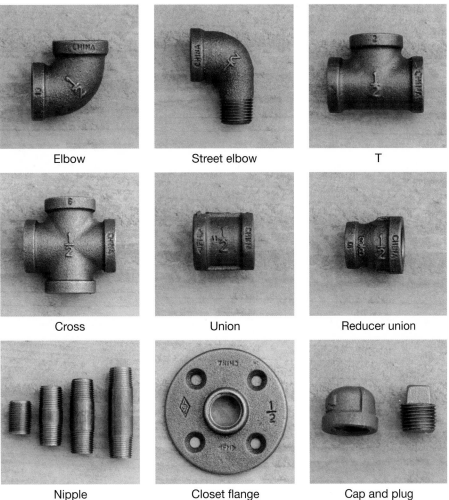

Elbow	Street elbow	T
Cross	Union	Reducer union
Nipple	Closet flange	Cap and plug

Cap and Plug: A cap closes a pipe. Pretty simple. It is attached to the male end of a pipe or fitting and it's a nice way to cover the sharp threads of an exposed pipe. A plug has a similar function as a cap, but inserts into the female end of a pipe or fitting and has a much neater look than a cap. It also has a very clean square knob that works well as a foot.

WHERE TO BUY

There are specialty plumbing supply retailers, but pretty much all of the mainstream hardware stores offer a decent selection too. If your store doesn't have what you need, it doesn't hurt to drive across the street and check out their competition. You might think that all hardware stores have the same inventory, but that's not necessarily true. Trust me on this; I've been to a lot of hardware stores buying pipes lately.

Still can't find what you need? Check online. There are several websites that stock a huge assortment of sizes and will cut what you need to order. If you're not in any hurry and you don't mind paying for shipping, this could be the route for you.

Just to make it a little easier, I tried to use pipe sizes that are readily available at major hardware stores for most of the projects in this book. You're welcome.

CUTTING PIPES

Most big hardware stores will cut and thread pipes for you on site. For free. All you have to do is ask…and probably wait. If you're really into building with pipes, I mean *really* into them, there are pipe cutters that you can buy. A small one is just a few hundred dollars. But honestly, how often are you going to use it? I say just wait for the guy at the hardware store.

CLEANING

You will probably notice that most plumbing pipes are covered in a sticky grease. If you have a pipe cut, the store will grease it even more when they rethread the end.

Use a sharp scraper with a fresh razor blade to scrape the store stickers off. Be sure to always push the blade away from you. To clean them afterward, I wash my pipes and fittings with orange hand cleaner from the auto parts store. Orange hand cleaner is a product mechanics use to remove grease and residue off their hands. There are several different brands, all made from oranges. It's the color orange, it's made from orange oils, and it smells like oranges. Any brand will work. It's amazing. It will take off all the sticky and all of the greasy.

TO PAINT OR NOT TO PAINT?

Good question. It won't take you long to notice that black pipe fittings aren't really black. They're more of a dark gray color. Doesn't bother me. I like the contrast.

If you decide to paint, it's best to do it once the piece is completed. Make sure that your pipes are clean of any residue, or the paint won't stick. Set your finished piece in a well-ventilated area. Use a good quality of spray paint. I know that 99-cent spray paint sounds like a great bargain, but a better-quality spray paint will cover much more smoothly and last longer. Position the can about 10 to 12 inches from the object, and move your arm back and forth as you spray. Give it several light coats. If your paint runs, you're spraying too heavily. Give everything a good amount of time to dry. No one wants to see your fingerprints.

SAFETY FIRST

The threaded ends of pipes are pretty sharp. That's why it's best to always handle them with gloves. Get a pair of rubber-palmed gloves. Not only will they protect your hands from the sharp edges, but they'll also help you get a good grip so you can twist all your connections together even more tightly.

I do realize that I'm not wearing gloves in most of the pictures in this book. That's because the pictures were so much more attractive without them. So "do as I say, not as I do," and protect your hands.

CUTTING WOOD

I know that you were expecting a book entirely on pipe, but industrial pipe and wood are natural complements. Like peanut butter and jelly. Most big hardware stores will cut your wood to size for you. You just have to ask and probably wait a little bit.

A small chop saw is a good investment if you plan to use it on a regular basis. If not, look into renting one. It costs about half of the purchase price to rent one for 24 hours.

STAINING YOUR WOOD

Once it's cut, you'll want to stain your wood for each project. Be sure to sand down any rough edges and wipe the whole piece with a clean rag to remove any loose sawdust. Wear rubber gloves—unless you want brown fingertips.

Use a clean cotton rag to wipe the stain on in the direction of the wood grain. Be sure to keep a "wet edge" as you stain. This just means to continue staining a board until the entire piece is stained. If you allow an area to dry and then go over it with more stain, the stain might build up and look messy. I know you don't want that.

BUY A DRILL

Every household should own a cordless drill. Why use a screwdriver when you can use an electric one? A reasonably priced drill, maybe about $50 to $60, can be bought at any hardware store. Keep the charger plugged in—and charging—in a storage closet. With a keyless chuck and your bare hands, you can change the drill from a screw bit to a drill bit quickly. Now it's twice as useful.

HANGING IT UP

Occasionally, you will want to hang your finished pipe pieces on the wall, and you probably won't want them to fall off. Fixtures like coat racks, hooks, or light sconces are easily attached to the wall with drywall anchors, or better yet, toggle bolts. Toggle bolts have little wings at the ends that open on the inside of the wall.

Small fixtures that won't be under very much stress can be hung with drywall anchors. Buy the metal anchors that screw directly into the drywall, and even wood, with a screwdriver. Simply use the included screw to hang your piece by screwing it directly into the anchor. It couldn't be easier.

Toggle bolts are best for heavy fixtures, or fixtures that will probably become heavy with coats or tools. Use a drill with a paddle bit to make a hole in the drywall. Push the wings of the toggle into the hole as far as you can so they have space to open fully. Pull the toggle toward you and screw it in. As you screw, the toggle becomes tighter and tighter until it won't move anymore. Congratulations, you've just attached your fixture to the wall.

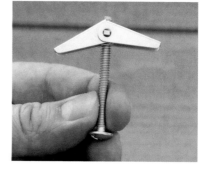

SIMPLE COAT PUCKS

When we were faced with a lack of good storage, I had to do something.

Our old house has very small closets and worst of all, no real mudroom. There was a small section of wall in the garage by the kitchen door that was just begging for some kind of storage solution.

My answer? Simple coat pucks.

SUPPLIES

Use ½-inch-diameter galvanized pipe and fittings.

- 7 caps
- 7 (2-inch) nipples

- 7 flanges
- 2-inch silver screws

TOOLS

- Cordless drill with screw bit

- Tape measure

Skill Level: **Easy**

Time: **10 minutes**

DIRECTIONS:

1. Twist a cap onto one end of the first pipe nipple.

2. Add the flange to the other end of the nipple. Repeat steps 1–2 six more times.

3. Attach the pucks directly into wood paneling using screws and a cordless drill. If you plan on hanging heavy coats or you're hanging the pucks directly onto drywall, you will probably want to use drywall anchors. (See page 12 for more on drywall anchors.)

4. Use the tape measure to space out all seven pucks at just about 5 inches apart from each other in a gridded diamond pattern.

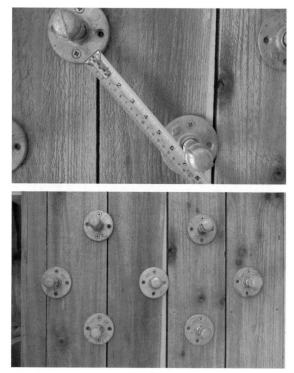

Now you have the perfect impromptu place to hang hats, bags, jackets, and even the dog leash before coming into the house. Hello, mudroom.

These could also work in the bathroom to hang towels on. Or maybe on the back of the bedroom door for robes. Heck, just about anywhere you need a hook.

PAPER TOWEL HOLDER

Don't you just love sloppy barbecue? I think you know the kind I mean: real barbecue, with sweet and smoky sauce that coats your fingers and maybe even your face. That's how you know it's the best. You know what would come in handy with those? A big roll of paper towels.

All the barbecue restaurants in Texas have one of these paper towel holders screwed down to every picnic table, keeping them right where you'd want them to be—in front of your face.

Here's a simple project to give you that same convenience without filling your kitchen table full of screw holes.

SUPPLIES

Use ½-inch-diameter galvanized pipe and fittings.

- 12-inch pipe

- Cap
- Flange
- Wood stain

- 6-inch wood disc
- ¾-inch silver screws
- Self-adhesive rubber bumpers

TOOLS

- Clean rag

- Drill with screw bit attachment

Skill Level: **Easy**

Time: **10 minutes, plus dry time**

DIRECTIONS:

1. Attach the cap to one end of the 12-inch-long pipe.

2. Screw the other end of the pipe into the flange.

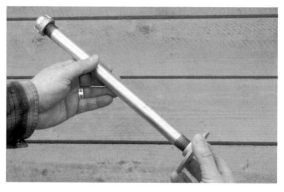

3. Use the rag to stain the wood disc in your choice of color. (I used American Walnut.) Allow to completely dry according to the package directions.

4. Screw the flange into the center of the wood disc with the ¾-inch silver screws.

5. Apply 4–5 self-adhesive rubber bumpers to the bottom of the wood disc to keep it from sliding when someone pulls a paper towel off.

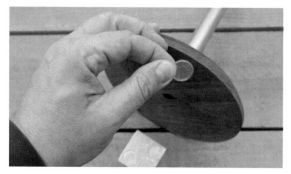

Place a roll of paper towels over the pipe and you're all set for an evening of eating messy barbecue. You'll find that this project comes in handy when eating other foods too. All of them, actually!

JEWELRY STAND

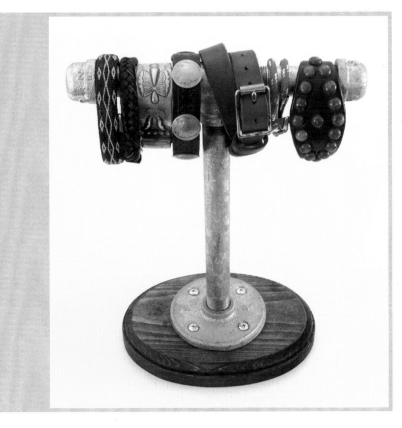

If you're anything like me (and I'm willing to bet that you are), you know the struggle of trying to find that one perfect accessory from a drawer filled with junk. Well, fear no more. The answer to your troubles is just a few pipe twists away.

SUPPLIES

Use ½-inch-diameter galvanized pipes and fittings.

- 2 cap fittings
- 2 (3-inch) nipples

- T fitting
- 8-inch nipple
- Flange

- 7-inch oval wood plaque
- Water-based gel wood stain
- ¾-inch silver screws

TOOLS

- Rubber gloves

- Cotton rag

- Electric drill with screw bit

Skill Level: **Easy**

Time: **Half hour**

DIRECTIONS: **FOR THE JEWELRY STAND**

1. Lay out all your pipe pieces.

2. Add the cap fittings to the two 3-inch-long nipples.

3. Attach the 3-inch nipples to the opposite ends of the T fitting.

4. Twist the 8-inch-long nipple to the bottom opening of the T.

5. Attach the flange to the bottom of the 8-inch nipple.

DIRECTIONS: **TO STAIN THE WOOD BASE**

1. Use water-based gel wood stain in your choice of color. My favorite brand is Minwax. I chose Onyx.

2. Apply a small amount to a dry cotton rag. (Wear latex gloves to protect your hands, even though the stain washes off with soap and water.)

3. Wipe the stain on and quickly wipe off any excess. Because the gel stain is water-based, it dries very quickly.

4. Use the drill and ¾-inch screws to attach your jewelry stand to the wood base.

TIP: Starting with just a small amount of stain will let more of the wood grain show through. You can always add more stain to make it darker, but you can't make it lighter.

TP HOLDER

This project has "summer camp" written all over it. Remember summer camp? The cabins, the mosquitoes, the bonfires, the *almost* public showers, badminton, swimming in a murky lake, poison ivy, hot dogs.

Toilet paper on a galvanized pipe holder should take you back to those rustic summers of your youth. Now that I've sold it, I give you a TP Holder.

SUPPLIES

Use ½-inch-diameter galvanized pipe and fittings.

- Flange
- 2-inch nipple
- 90-degree elbow
- 5-inch nipple
- Cap
- ¾-inch silver screws

TOOLS

- Cordless drill with screw bit

Skill Level: **Easy**

Time: **10 minutes**

DIRECTIONS:

1. Lay out all the pieces in the shape of a right angle as follows: flange, 2-inch nipple, elbow, 5-inch nipple and cap.

2. Connect the flange to the 2-inch-long nipple.

3. Add the elbow to the top of the 2-inch-long nipple.

4. Finish the assembly with the 5-inch-long nipple and the cap.

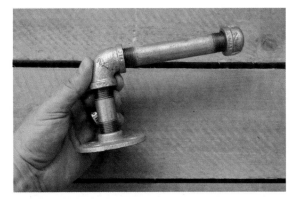

5. Screw it on where it needs to be with the silver screws.

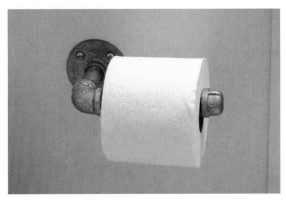

It's actually pretty functional and simple to make.

RED VALVE COAT RACK

Several years ago, when I tried to follow the hostess at a restaurant, I found that I couldn't move. I had been leaning against the wall waiting for the next available table.

I was wearing my favorite denim jacket. The denim jacket that was a birthday present for my eighteenth birthday—the day before. The very jacket that I had been coveting for months. I had to peel it off the wall. The wall that had been freshly painted Kelly green.

I loathe Kelly green walls.

An obscene amount of jackets later, I'm still trying to replace that one with the streak of green paint across the back. I need someplace to keep all those jackets. How about an industrial coat rack made from red valves?

SUPPLIES

Use ½-inch-diameter black pipes and fittings.

- 5 red-handled gate valves

- Metallic spray paint
- 2 (90-degree) street elbows
- 2 flanges

- 2 (2-inch) nipples
- 4 (5-inch) nipples
- 2 (2-inch) toggle bolts

TOOLS

- Level
- Pliers

- Electric drill with a screw bit and ½-inch paddle bit

Skill Level: **Intermediate**   Time: **1 hour**

DIRECTIONS: **FOR THE RACK**

1. Remove the red knob from the first gate valve by unscrewing the hex nut with a pair of pliers. Throw away the green washer part with the manufacturing info on it. It's not attractive, and we're going for attractive. Repeat with remaining valves, setting the red handles aside.

2. Lay the valve pieces in a well-ventilated area, on a drop cloth, and apply a few light coats of metallic spray paint. (Because black pipe fittings aren't *exactly* black, Flat Soft Iron from Rust-Oleum is the best paint color to match.) Don't forget to spray the hex nuts too. Allow to dry well before handling.

TIP: Gate valves are exactly what they sound like: pipe valves that act as gates for water to pass, or not pass, through. If you've ever turned on an outdoor faucet, and I'm willing to bet that you have, you've used a gate valve.

Unfortunately, they are easiest to find in copper. But the rest of our pipe pieces are iron-colored. Not a problem.

3. Attach the street elbows to the flanges.

4. Measure the distance from the flange to the top of elbow. It should be the same on each piece: just about 2 inches. If the distances aren't close, the finished rack won't lie flat against the wall.

5. Add the 2-inch-long nipples to each elbow.

6. Start adding the valve pieces and the 5-inch-long nipples, alternating as you go and finishing with the other flange/elbow piece. Make sure all the valves are aimed up and the connections are as tight as possible.

7. Reattach the red handles to every valve with the hex nut.

8. Make sure your finished rack lies flat and you're finished.

DIRECTIONS: **TO HANG THE FINISHED RACK**

1. Using the level, hold your coat rack in place on the wall and mark the top hole of each flange with a pencil.

2. The toggle bolt package will usually say what size drill bit to use to make the hole. If it doesn't, or you just want to be sure, pinch the toggle ends together and match them up with a drill bit that looks about the same size. My toggle bolts call for a ½-inch paddle bit.

3. With the proper size drill bit attached, drill into the pencil mark. If you feel some resistance after drilling in about a quarter inch, congratulations, you've found a stud. (In a newly built home, there should be a stud every 16 inches.) You can use a regular

TIP: Because iron pipe is pretty heavy, and your rack will probably hold several heavy coats, you'll want to make sure it's securely on the wall. The best way to do this is with toggle bolts.

screw to hang your rack. But chances are pretty high that you will just find air and then you will need to use a toggle bolt.

4. Unscrew the wings on the toggle bolt. Slip the bolt through the flange hole and re-screw the wings on the other side of the flange. Pinch the wings shut and push them into the ½-inch wall hole as far as they will go.

5. Pull the rack toward you and the toggle wings will open and latch on the other side of the drywall. With a cordless drill, screw the bolt in while gently pulling the fixture away from the wall. As you screw, the distance will shorten as the bolt tightens from inside.

6. Repeat the toggle bolt process with the flange on the other side of the rack. If the rack looks unlevel, it's simply a matter of loosening the bolt a little, making the adjustment, and retightening the bolt. When you're certain your rack is completely level, tighten both bolts as well as you can.

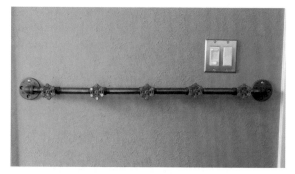

Your rack is finished and ready for coats. It's almost a shame to cover it. But all those coats have got to go somewhere. Hopefully not leaning against a freshly painted wall.

GARDEN TOOL RACK

I'm comfortable inside the house installing can lights or tiling a bathroom, but Jamie's usually the one outside getting his hands dirty.

In just a few short years, he's altered everything that we didn't like about our bland yard. He's replaced all the boring shrubs with a rock-lined, lush landscape of agave, rosemary, yucca, and sage. At the first sign of spring, he's at every garden center searching out my favorite flowers: Indian blankets, marigolds, and Coreopsis 'Salsa'. He's dug drainage, carted in boulders, trimmed trees, power-washed the driveway, mowed the lawn every weekend (diagonally, of course), and even designed/supervised the deck of our dreams.

What better thank you than to help him organize those garden tools in a stylish manner?

SUPPLIES

Use ¾-inch-diameter galvanized pipe.

- 2 x 4 x 40-inch cedar plank
- Brown stain

- 6 (4-inch) pipes
- 6 caps

TOOLS

- Rubber mallet

- Cordless drill

- ¹⁵/₁₆-inch paddle bit

Skill Level: **Easy**

Time: **1 hour**

DIRECTIONS:

1. Stain the cedar plank in your choice of stain and allow it to dry thoroughly. My fence and tool shed are both cedar, so I stained my board a matching shade of warm, russet brown.

2. Screw the caps onto the ends of the 6 pipes.

TIP: Cedar is a beautifully textured wood that's easy to work with because it's lightweight. Unfortunately, it also absorbs water, causing it to expand. So, if there's a chance of your rack getting rained on, it's probably better to use pressure-treated lumber.

3. Position a tool where you will want it to hang on the cedar plank and place a pipe on either side of it. With a rubber mallet, give each pipe a good pound.

4. Cedar is so soft that the pipes will leave a perfect impression, showing exactly where to drill your holes.

5. Choose a paddle bit that is the same size as your pipe. For ¾-inch pipe, a ¹⁵/₁₆-inch paddle bit works perfectly. Remember that ¾-inch refers to the *inside* diameter of the pipe.

6. Use a cordless drill fitted with the ¹⁵/₁₆-inch paddle bit to drill out holes for the pipes. Be sure to push straight down.

7. Your holes should be just about an inch deep. If they aren't deep enough, the pipes won't be strong enough to support your heavy tools.

8. Use a rubber mallet to pound the pipes into the holes. Be sure to keep them as straight as possible.

9. Of course it completely depends on the size of the tools you intend to hang, but the pipes should be mounted just about 2 inches apart.

10. Continue adding the remaining pipes. Depending on the size and type of tools, the distance between them should be about 12 inches.

Hang your finished rack where you'll need it the most, and load it with a few big gardening implements. Maybe now I'll be more likely to pitch in with the yard work and get my hands dirty. But probably not.

PLUMBING PIPE CLOTHES RACK

I had a walk-in closet in my first college dorm room. Can you believe that? It was roomy enough to hide five tipsy frat brothers from the RA. I didn't realize how great I had it back then.

Flash forward a few decades to the 1970s ranch house I live in currently, with just two little closets and a wardrobe big enough to dress a small nation. This rolling closet was a must to handle some of the overflow. It's also the ideal rack to use in a mudroom for coats and jackets, in the laundry room for hanging clothes as soon as they come out of the dryer, or as an additional mobile, open-air closet. The lower two bars are perfect storage for boots and shoes.

SUPPLIES

Use ½-inch-diameter black pipe and fittings.

- 6 T fittings
- 4 close nipples
- 4 (2-inch) nipples
- 6 elbows
- 4 (8-inch) pipes
- 4 flanges
- 5 4-foot pipes
- 3 (2 x 6 x 53-inch) pine boards
- 3 (1 x 4 x 16-inch) pine boards
- Brown stain
- 1½-inch black drywall screws
- 6 (2-inch) black swivel casters

TOOLS

Cordless drill with screw bit

Skill Level: **Advanced**   Time: **About 3 hours**

DIRECTIONS: **FOR THE RACK**

1. Attach two of the close nipples to the sides of a T fitting.

2. Attach two of the T fittings to the close nipples by the side holes. The center T should be aimed up; the side T's should both aim forward.

3. Now twist in a 2-inch-long nipple to the side opening of each of the newly added T fittings.

4. Add an elbow to the ends of each of the 2-inch-long nipples and aim them both down.

5. Twist an 8-inch-long pipe into the downward opening of each elbow.

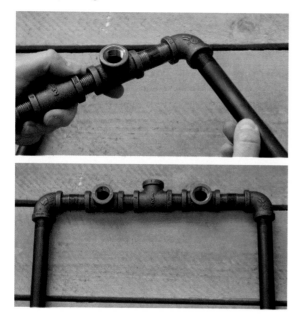

6. A flange twisted onto the end of each 8-inch-long pipe is the final piece.

7. Repeat the above steps to make a second footing assembly.

8. Attach a 4-foot-long pipe into each of the side T openings on one of the footing assemblies.

9. Connect the opposite ends of the 4-foot-long pipes to the other footing assembly. You will have to slightly unscrew the pipes from the side that you just connected. It will take some work, screwing back and forth, but eventually both sides will be connected to each other.

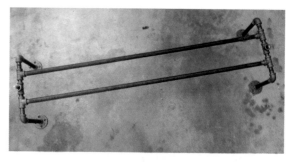

10. Add an elbow fitting to each end of another 4-foot-long pipe. This will be your hanging rack.

11. Then, add another 4-foot-long pipe to each elbow to create the sides of your hanging rack.

12. Push the bottom of each of these pipes into the finished footing. In order to screw into the lower footing piece, you will have to slightly unscrew from the top elbow. It will take a little work; much like connecting the two footing pieces together did. But it will happen.

DIRECTIONS: **FOR THE BASE**

1. Stain all the boards in your choice of stain. I used Minwax Jacobean. Allow the boards to dry thoroughly according to the directions on the can.

2. Position the three 2 x 6s as close together as possible and lay one of the 1 x 4s on top just near the edge. There should be about a quarter inch of larger board showing on three sides. Attach this board to the three larger boards with six or more drywall screws, straight down the middle.

3. Attach the swivel casters to the ends of the 1 x 4 with drywall screws.

4. Repeat adding casters to the ends of the other two support boards.

5. Flip the wood base over onto the casters.

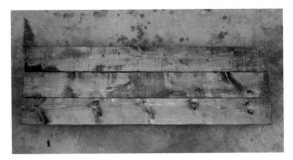

6. Position the pipe frame on top of the wood base.

7. Use more drywall screws and the drill to attach the pipe frame to the wood base.

ROLLING LOG HOLDER

This is the project that started my love of building with industrial plumbing pipes.

We have a gas fireplace, and everyone knows that gas-burning fireplaces are practical. They're easy to light, require absolutely no wood, and don't leave behind a gallon of dirty ash. But where's the romance in that? I'd much rather burn wood. There is absolutely no denying that the crackle and pop of wood burning sets everyone's emotions into overdrive. And don't discount the heavenly aroma either. Burning hickory or piñon logs smells like summer camp and Christmas all rolled into one. Makes our whole house manly fragrant. Gas fires just can't offer that.

So where do you efficiently keep all that firewood in the house? And how do you get it from the car to the fireplace in one easy trip? This log holder is the clever solution to both those problems. It takes up very little floor space and rolls a heavy load like a dream.

SUPPLIES

Use ¾-inch-diameter black pipes and fittings.

- 2 (2 x 4 x 10½-inch) pine boards
- 2 (2 x 4 x 19½-inch) pine boards,
- 2 (2 x 4 x 13½-inch) pine boards
- 2 (2 x 4 x 22½ inch) pine boards
- 2½-inch drywall screws
- 2 (1 x 4 x 24-inch) pine board with mitered edges
- 2 (1 x 4 x 24-inch) pine board with mitered edges
- 2 (¾ x 18 x 24-inch) pieces of birch plywood
- Minwax Jacobean Stain

- 4 (4-inch) casters (two with locks)
- 2-inch lag screws

- 2 T fittings
- 18-inch pipe
- 4 (5-inch) pipes

- 4 elbows
- 4 (60-inch) pipes
- 4 flanges

TOOLS

- Electric chop saw (optional)
- Cordless drill with a screw bit

- ⅛-inch drill bit
- Hex socket bit
- Nail gun

- Clean cotton rag
- Rubber gloves
- Tape measure

Skill Level: **Advanced**   Time: **About 2 hours**

DIRECTIONS: **FOR THE BOX**

1. Because the weight of all that firewood can put stress on your pipes, it's important to have a sturdy base for the pipe assembly to connect to. Cut the eight 2 x 4s for the center of the box. If you don't have an electric chop saw, a small one is a pretty good household investment, most chain hardware stores will cut wood to size. For free. You just have to ask.

2. Start the center of the box with the 10½-inch and the 19½-inch boards. The shorter boards are the sides. They go in between the longer ones, which are the front and back.

3. Predrill pilot holes for drywall screws into the edges of the 19½-inch boards with a ⅛-inch drill bit.

4. Using the drill with the screw bit, screw the 2 x 4s together with 2½-inch drywall screws. It doesn't have to be perfect, or even pretty, because this is just the framework for the rest of the box. But a nice, tight connection of the boards is best.

5. With more pilot holes and drywall screws, add the remaining 2 x 4s to the outside of this finished box. The 13½-inch boards are the sides, and the 22½-inch boards are the front and back.

6. Line up the 1 x 4s for the sides of the box.

7. Attach the sides with a nail gun. If you don't have a nail gun, you can use finishing nails. You'll just have to countersink the nail heads.

8. Lay the ¾-inch-thick plywood pieces on the top and bottom of the box and attach these with the nail gun as well.

9. Stain the entire box a deep, rich brown color. I prefer Minwax Jacobean. Use a clean cotton rag and be sure to protect your hands with rubber gloves. Allow the box to dry according to the directions on the can.

10. Determine which side will be the front of the box. Use lag screws and a cordless drill with a hex socket bit to attach the casters with locks to the bottom of the box. (Be sure to predrill pilot holes for the lag screws) The unlocking casters will be at the back of the box.

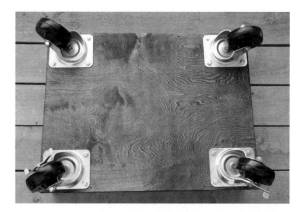

DIRECTIONS: **BUILDING THE PIPE FRAME**

1. Connect a T fitting to each end of the 18-inch-long pipe.

3. Add the four 5-inch-long pipes to the sides of the T fittings.

2. Be sure that the distance between the two fitting is about 17¼ inches.

4. Twist on the elbows to the ends of each of these pipes. Be sure to aim them all up.

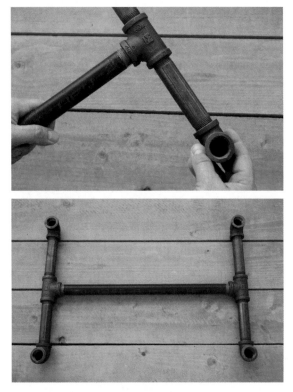

5. Now, connect each of the 60-inch pipes to these elbows.

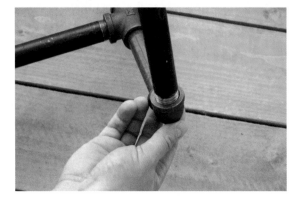

6. Cap these with the flanges.

7. Flip the pipe fixture over and position it on top of the wooden box. Attach the flanges with lag screws. (Anytime you use lag screws, be sure to drill pilot holes first.)

Your log holder is ready to be loaded with firewood and let the romance begin.

WALL-MOUNTED CANDLE SCONCE

If you're new to working with industrial plumbing pipes and you happen to like candles, this might be just the project for you.

It's inexpensive, oh so simple, and offers up plenty of drama. I've scattered these sconces down a pretty dismal hallway for an instant industrial/medieval look. I've even attached them to the fence line across our backyard for parties.

SUPPLIES

Use ½-inch-diameter black pipes and fittings.

- T fitting
- 2 (2½-inch) nipples
- Cap
- 2 flanges
- 1½-inch nipple
- Black drywall screws
- 4-inch candle

TOOLS

- Cordless drill with screw bit for hanging

Skill Level: **Easy**   Time: **10 minutes**

DIRECTIONS:

1. Lay out the T fitting, 2½-inch-long nipples, cap, flanges, and 1½-inch-long nipple.

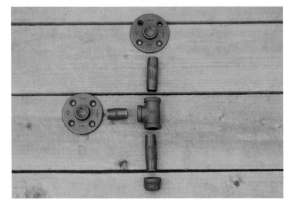

2. Attach the 2½-inch-long nipples to either side of the T fitting.

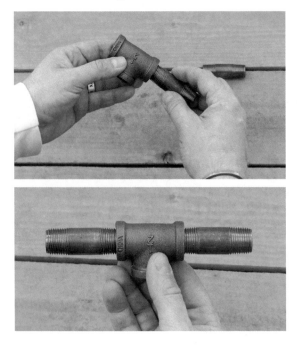

3. Screw on the cap fitting at one end of the extended T piece.

4. Twist on a flange at the other end.

5. Attach the 1½-inch-long nipple to the center of the T fitting.

6. Add the remaining flange to the end of the nipple.

7. Simply use black drywall screws to attach your sconce to the wall. Place a 4-inch candle on top, and enjoy your new industrial sconce and, of course, the mood it will instantly create.

INDUSTRIAL CANDELABRA

Remember those old black-and-white horror movies? The kind where a mad scientist with a creepy little mustache lives in a decrepit old mansion? It's always the only house for miles. An unsuspecting young couple, chased by something unseen, runs through the pouring rain to the front door of the mansion. There's thunder, a flash of lightning, and then a shriek as Vincent Price opens the door holding a candelabra.

I'll bet Mr. Price never imagined a candelabra quite like this one. It's a little bit industrial. It's a little bit traditional. And it's a ton of cool.

SUPPLIES

Use ⅜-inch-diameter black pipes and fittings.

- 8 T fittings
- 6 (2-inch) nipples
- 3 close nipples

- 5 (½ to ⅜-inch) reducing couplings
- 6-inch nipple
- 2 (4-inch) nipples
- 6 (2½-inch) nipples

- 5 caps
- 2 (2-inch) nipples
- Union
- 5 taper candles

Skill Level: **Intermediate**   Time: **About 15 minutes**

DIRECTIONS:

1. Add a T fitting to either end of a 2-inch-long nipple.

2. Add a close nipple to the bottom opening of each T fitting.

3. Twist on a T fitting to each close nipple. Don't tighten these pieces too tightly. You'll want to angle them when the piece is assembled.

4. Add a 2-inch-long nipple to the side opening of each of these T fittings.

5. Add another T fitting to the ends of each 2-inch-long nipple.

6. On the left side of the assembly, add another T fitting using a close nipple. Don't tighten this piece too tightly either.

7. To this newly added T fitting, attach a 2-inch-long nipple.

8. Finish off the left side of the candelabra assembly with the last T fitting.

9. To make the stems, attach a reducing coupling to the tops of the 6-inch-long, two 4-inch-long, and two of the 2½-inch-long nipples.

10. Screw each of these pieces to the top of the candelabra assembly. You'll want to stagger the heights of each pipe piece so that your candles will be different heights.

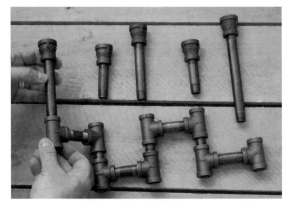

11. Make four of the feet out of the remaining 2½-inch-long pipes by adding the caps to the bottoms. Screw each of these feet into the four T fittings on the right side.

12. Three-eighths-inch pipes aren't as common as other sizes, so there are fewer options. Because the far left leg is a different height, and I'm using off-the-shelf pipes, I have to make the correct length with two 2-inch nipples, a union, and a cap.

13. Attach this last leg to the to the open T fitting.

14. To make the finished candelabra stand up, simply angle the T connections (remember that we left them a little loose) so that the feet zigzag.

Add a tall taper candle to each coupling and you're all finished. Of course, this one works best stationary. Not so much for carrying around in a blackout.

TIP: You can use an extra reducing coupling to "sharpen" the candles to make them stand. Just twist the coupling around the bottom of each candle to remove some of the wax.

HANGING WALL PENDANT

These dangling light fixtures seem to be everywhere these days. Just the other day, a dear friend and I were sitting under one at a hip restaurant. It was one of those cool new places with farm-to-table cuisine, a wait staff that looked like Civil War deserters, and a craft beer menu 10 times longer than the food menu. As my friend nibbled at her heirloom tomato and mascarpone tart with a cilantro pesto dribble, I could tell that she was overly impressed by all of it.

I wasn't. When she commented on how elaborate the light fixtures looked, I just had to roll my eyes, because I know that I could make one. In fact, I'm fairly certain that I could *show* someone how to make one.

SUPPLIES

Use ½-inch-diameter black pipe and fittings.

- Hanging pendant light kit with a working switch on the socket
- 45-degree street elbow
- 2 (18-inch) pipes
- 2 45-degree elbows
- 12-inch pipe
- 3 close nipples
- 2 90-degree elbows
- 2 flanges
- 8-inch pipe
- Reducing T fitting (½-inch to ¾-inch on side)
- 3-inch nipple
- T fitting
- Fabric-covered extension cord
- ¾ to ½-inch compression adapter
- 2 wire nuts
- Drywall anchors with screws
- Large round Edison-style lightbulb

TOOLS

- Tape measure
- Needle-nose pliers
- Scissors
- Black electrical tape
- Cordless drill with screw bit

Skill Level: **Intermediate**   Time: **2 hours**

DIRECTIONS:

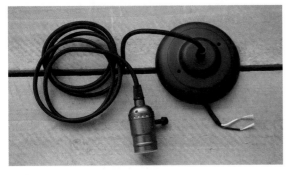

1. My hanging pendant light kit is meant to be hard-wired into a ceiling mount. Remove the ceiling plate by loosening the bolt with pliers and pulling the lamp cord out. (If your kit has a plug and not a ceiling plate, simply cut the plug off with scissors.)

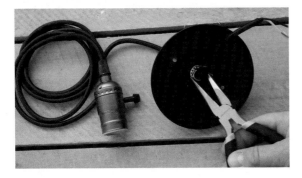

2. Push the lamp cord through the smaller end of the 45-degree street elbow fitting.

3. Start building the lamp arm by attaching an 18-inch-long pipe to the end of the street elbow. Continue to pull the lamp cord through.

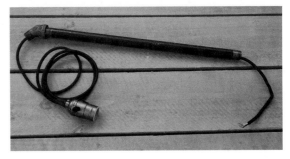

4. Complete the lamp arm by adding a 45-degree elbow, a 12-inch-long pipe, and the second 45-degree elbow.

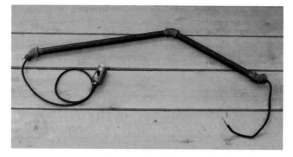

5. To make the footings for the wall mount, insert close nipples into the 90-degree elbows. Then attach the elbows to the flanges.

6. In order for the wall mount to rest flush on the wall, and you will want it to, be sure that the two elbow units are the same height, just about 3¼ inches.

7. Continue building the wall mount by adding the 8-inch-long pipe to one of the footing elbow units and the reducing T fitting with a 3-inch-long nipple to the other.

8. The 8-inch-long pipe will be at the top of the wall mount bracket, so attach the T fitting with a remaining close nipple to the open end of the pipe. Because you'll want this connection to swing, tighten the T fitting loosely.

9. Thread the lamp cord through the close nipple and out the bottom of the T fitting.

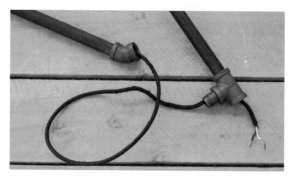

10. Thread the remaining lamp cord through the second 18-inch-long pipe.

11. Tighten the pipes around the lamp cord. Make the connection between the 45-degree elbow and the close nipple as tight as possible, so the lamp arm stays upright, but remember to leave the T fitting on the wall mount a little loose.

12. Push the cord through the top opening of the reducing T fitting in the bottom piece of the wall-mount assembly, and pull it out of the ¾-inch side with needle-nose pliers.

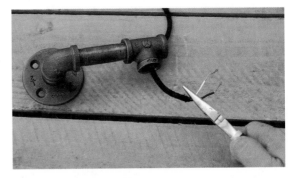

13. Tighten the connections of the wall mount. The opening of the T fitting should aim slightly backward.

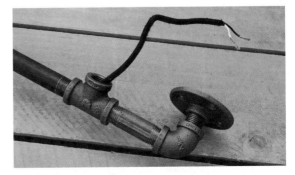

14. Extension cords are the perfect power cord for homemade lamps. They already have the male end attached. Simply use a pair of scissors to cut off the female end of the cord.

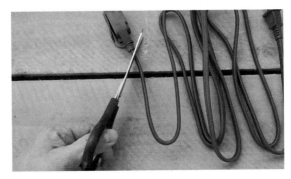

15. Slide the compression adapter down the cut cord, small end first. With the scissors, cut back a few inches of the fabric covering. Then, split the inner wires and cut back an inch of plastic to expose the copper wires underneath.

16. Twist the lamp cord wires together with the extension cord wires. Be sure to keep each side separated.

17. Protect the connections with wire nuts and wrap each side separately in black electrical tape.

18. Push all the wires and connections into the open end of the T fitting and slide the compression adapter up the power cord. Tighten the compression adapter.

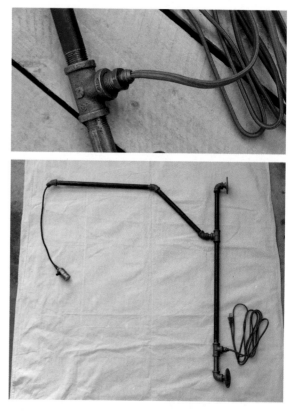

19. Use drywall anchors to hang your new lamp.

20. Mark the flange holes on the wall with a pencil and drill the anchors in just like they were screws.

21. Line up the holes on the flanges with the holes in the anchors, and screw in screws.

Add a large round Edison-style lightbulb. Pull a table under your new pendant lamp and enjoy some artisanal bacon-kale jam.

STEAMPUNK FLOOR LAMP

I've always loved the look of reclaimed industrial lamps. Too bad they're so expensive.

When I discovered the "convert a bottle into a lamp" kit at the hardware store the hamster on a wheel in my brain started running full speed. With a socket and a cord, now anything could become a lamp. Seriously, anything. Not just glass bottles, like the kit is intended for, but even a pile of pipes.

SUPPLIES

Use ½-inch-diameter black pipes and fittings (unless noted).

- 2 (5-gallon) pickle buckets
- 2 (8-inch) pipes
- Flange
- ¾ to ½-inch reducing T fitting
- 10-pound bag of fast-drying cement
- Lamp kit for a bottle lamp
- ¾ to ½-inch bushing coupling
- 1 to ¾-inch reducing union
- 2 T fittings
- Close nipple
- 6-inch pipe
- Elbow fitting
- 10-inch pipe
- 2½-inch pipe
- 2 caps
- 3-foot pipe
- ¾ to ⅜-inch compression adapter

- Black fabric-covered extension cord
- Small wire nuts
- Lamp cage
- Edison-style 40-watt lightbulb

TOOLS

- Tape measure
- Pencil
- Blue painter's tape
- Nonstick cooking spray
- Big stick to stir cement

- Rubber gloves
- 4-inch putty knife
- Screwdriver
- Flat metallic soft iron spray paint
- Box cutter, if needed

- Heavy grit sandpaper, if needed
- Needle-nose pliers
- Scissors
- Black electrical tape

Skill Level: **Advanced**   Time: **About 2 hours, plus cement-drying time**

DIRECTIONS:

1. Mark the inside of the pickle bucket with a pencil at 4 inches from the bottom.

3. Screw the 8-inch-long pipe into the flange.

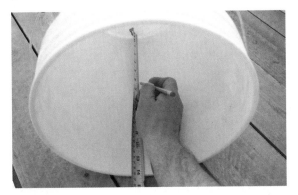

2. Run a few lines of painter's tape above the 4-inch marks. This will be your guide for the height of the cement.

4. Connect the reducing T fitting to the top of the 8-inch-long pipe. The side opening is where the power cord will exit the finished lamp.

5. Attach a wad of painter's tape to the bottom of the flange. It doesn't need to be a lot, just enough to keep it in place.

6. Stick the flange to the center of the bucket.

7. Spray the inside of the bucket with a light coating of cooking spray. This brilliant tip will help remove the hardened cement once it dries. It will also help remove any excess cement you may spread onto the pipe.

8. In the second bucket, mix the quick-dry cement according to the package directions. Usually, a 10-pound bag of cement requires about 2 cups of water, but you may have to add a little bit more if your mixture is too stiff. Always add the dry cement mix to the water, and not the other way around or it will be lumpy. Use a thick stick to stir with, and wear gloves to protect your hands. You'll know the cement is ready when it's the consistency of oatmeal.

9. Transfer the mixed cement to the first bucket with the putty knife a few scoops at a time. Smooth it around the pipe and try to get it as level as you can using the blue tape as a guide.

10. Lay out the pieces in the lamp kit. A typical lamp kit for converting a bottle into a lamp will contain: a lamp cord, a socket with an on/off switch, a socket shell, a check ring,

a threaded rod, and a few ribbed rubber spacers.

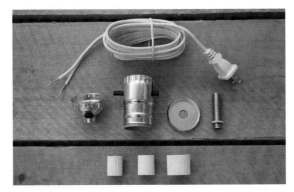

11. Insert a tight fitting rubber spacer into the threaded end of the bushing coupling.

12. Push the threaded rod into the white ribbed bushing as snugly as you can with your hands. This will hold your lamp socket securely inside the coupling.

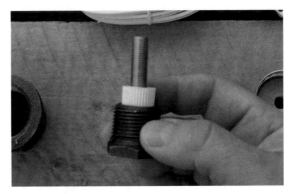

13. Screw the reducing coupling straight down onto the bushing coupling and the threaded lamp rod.

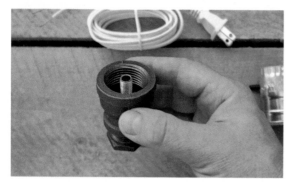

14. Screw the bottom of the socket cap from the lamp kit onto the threaded rod inside the reducing coupling. Twist it as far down as it will go.

15. Push the cut end of the lamp cord into the threaded lamp rod through the bottom of the socket assembly.

16. Slide the socket cover forward to expose the screws on either side. Attach the cord wires to the screws with a screwdriver and slide the cover back down.

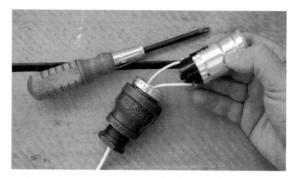

17. Gently push the socket pieces together and pull the excess cord through the back of the assembly. Give the outside of the lamp assembly a good spritz of the flat metallic soft iron spray paint to match the other fittings.

18. With a pair of scissors, cut the male end off the lamp cord. It's OK. It's not plugged in.

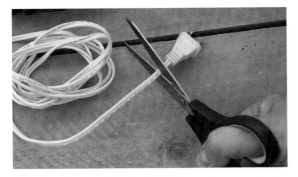

19. Lay out the 8-inch-long pipe, two T fittings, the close nipple, the 6-inch-long pipe, and an elbow fitting.

20. Thread the lamp cord through the pipe pieces. It's probably easier to thread and attach each fitting one at a time, but I wanted to show the order for assembly.

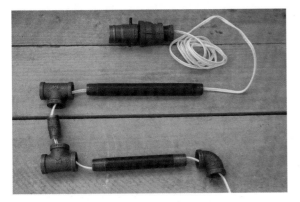

21. Tighten the pipes and fittings together and pull all of the excess lamp cord through.

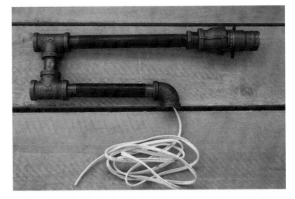

22. Add the 10-inch-long pipe with a cap to the open end of the T fitting on the top lamp arm, and add the 2½-inch-long pipe with a cap to the open end of the T fitting on the bottom lamp arm.

23. Once the cement for the lamp base is completely dry, probably about 24 hours, gently lift the base from the bucket. The cooking spray should have done the trick. If it does stick, don't panic. Simply use a box cutter to cut the bucket off the concrete base. You can use a heavy grit sandpaper to smooth out any rough spots.

24. Attach the 3-foot pipe into the top of the reducing T fitting in the top of the lamp base.

25. Push the lamp cord through the top of the 3-foot pipe in the base.

26. Use a pair of needle-nose pliers to gently pull the lamp cord through the side hole of the T fitting. Be careful not to puncture the cord with the pliers.

27. A compression adapter is the perfect fitting to extract your lamp cord. They are easiest to find in brass, so just give it a shot of flat metallic soft iron spray paint so it will match all of the other pipe fittings.

28. For the power cord, use a pair of scissors to cut off the female end of the fabric-covered extension cord. For safety reasons, make sure it's not plugged in.

29. Thread the newly painted compression adapter over the cut end of the fabric-covered extension cord small end first.

30. Use a pair of scissors to cut back some of the fabric covering from the cut end of the extension cord, then split the inner cord in half about 3 inches. Strip back the white plastic to expose the copper wires underneath on both sides.

31. Connect the power cord wires to the lamp wires by twisting the copper ends together. It doesn't matter which side is connected to which, just be sure to keep the two wires separated and not touching.

32. Use wire nuts and electrical tape to secure the wire connections. If you're worried about being shocked when the lamp is on, don't be. As long as these connections are grounded, or covered in plastic or tape, there's not a chance. There isn't enough power running through a lamp to hurt anyone anyway. It's more of an irritating tickle. Trust me, I've felt it.

33. Push the connected wires into the T fitting. Slide the compression adapter up the fabric cord and screw it into the open hole of the T fitting.

34. Attach the elbow on the top part of the lamp to the 3-foot pipe as tightly as you can.

35. Use a screwdriver to attach the lamp cage to the lamp socket.

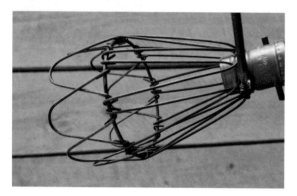

36. Insert an Edison-style lightbulb into the socket and close the cage.

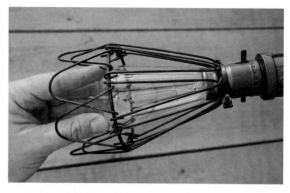

37. Plug it in, and switch the light on.

Pat yourself on the back because you just built an awesome steampunk floor lamp.

That wasn't so hard, now was it? I told you that I'd walk you through it.

TABLETOP LAMP

A few years ago we took a trip to Key West and the hotel booked us into a room with two twin beds. It was all they had. I know. Not a very romantic vacation. But we both agreed that having our own beds *was* a vacation. It was a little bit like summer camp.

The shared nightstand between the twin beds had a two-headed lamp. Each light was independent of the other. I liked the fact that I could read while Jamie was sleeping. This is my "industrial" version of that two-headed lamp.

SUPPLIES

Use ½-inch-diameter galvanized pipe and fittings.

- 2 (2½-inch) nipples
- 6 T fittings
- 5 close nipples
- 5 (90-degree) elbows
- 4 (½-inch) white rubber-leg tips
- 2 (5-inch) galvanized flower pots
- 2 make-a-lamp-in-a-bottle kits with pull chains
- 2 flanges
- 4¾-inch galvanized washers
- 2 (45-degree) elbows
- 2 (2-inch) nipples
- 3½-inch nipple
- 6-inch pipe
- Red-and-white fabric-covered extension cord
- ½ to ⅜-inch compression adapter
- Small wire nuts
- Plug fitting
- 2½-inch nipple
- ½-inch gate valve with red handle
- 5-inch pipe
- 2 small Edison-style lightbulbs

TOOLS

- Tape measure
- Sharpie
- Awl
- Hammer
- Tin snips
- Tissue
- Flat silver spray paint
- Screwdriver
- Scissors
- Pliers

Skill Level: **Advanced**   Time: **2 hours**

DIRECTIONS:

1. To make the legs for the lamp, first attach a 2½-inch-long nipple to each side of a T fitting.

2. Screw two more T fittings to the end of each 2½-inch-long nipple.

3. Add four close nipples to the side openings of the T fittings.

4. Attach four 90-degree elbows to the close nipples. Aim all four downward to make the feet.

5. Rubber-leg tips are generally sold to prevent metal folding chairs from scratching wood floors, but they'll work perfectly as stabilizers for a lamp too. Gently push the four rubber-leg tips into the open bottoms of the elbows and flip the unit over.

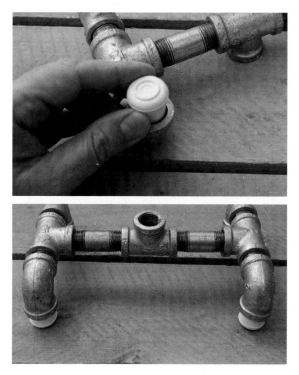

6. Most craft stores will sell small galvanized flower pots. They make perfect lamp shades for a piece like this. Flip it over and mark the center of the bottom with a Sharpie.

7. The tin is pretty thin and easy to puncture with an awl or even a screwdriver. Just give the tool a sharp tap with a hammer.

8. Trace a pipe nipple with a Sharpie around the center hole. They are all the same diameter, so it doesn't matter which one.

9. Use a pair of tin snips to cut the circle out of the bottom of the pot. Be careful, the newly cut and slightly jagged tin can be sharp.

10. Most hardware stores sell kits for making a bottle into a lamp. These kits usually contain a few feet of lamp cord, a socket with either a switch or a chain pull (you will want the chain pull for this lamp), a cap for the bottom of the socket, a washer, a threaded rod, and a few rubber spacers.

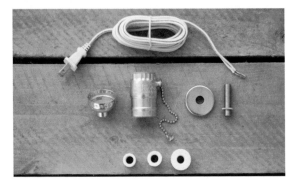

11. Brass is a perfectly fine finish, but not for this project. Stuff a piece of tissue into each socket to keep them from getting painted. Lay the sockets and socket caps in a well-ventilated area and spritz with flat silver spray paint. Allow to dry completely.

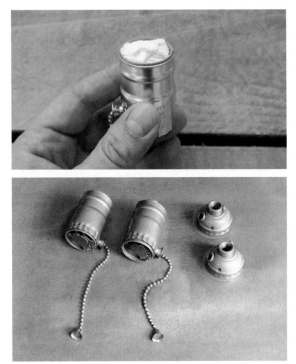

12. Insert a close nipple into the underside of a flange and tighten it as much as you can.

13. Twist the threaded rod from the lamp kit into the medium-sized rubber spacer.

14. Push the spacer/rod combo into the center of the flange with the close nipple under it.

15. Attach the socket cap to the rod by simply screwing it on.

16. Cut the male end off of the lamp cord. You won't need it, so just toss it. Thread the lamp cord through the bottom of the brass rod and out of the center of the socket cap.

17. Slide the cover for the lamp socket gently upward, revealing the brass screws underneath. Use a screwdriver to attach the wires from the lamp cord. One wire connected to each screw.

18. Slide the cover back over the screws and wires and gently push the socket into the socket cap. They should snap together nicely.

19. Slide a ¾-inch washer up the lamp cord and onto the close nipple on the underside of the lamp assembly.

20. Thread the lamp cord through the inside of the tin flowerpot, a second washer, a 45-degree elbow, and a 2-inch-long nipple.

22. Combine a T fitting, a 3½-inch nipple, and the final 90-degree elbow to create the neck of the lamp. Thread the lamp wires from each flower pot into either side of the T fitting and out the elbow together.

21. Tighten all the pieces together, holding the lamp assembly inside the flower pot. Then, repeat the above steps to make a second lamp head.

23. Attach the nipples on each flower pot to the T fitting and tighten.

24. Thread the lamp wire through the 6-inch-long pipe and another T fitting. Attach the 6-inch pipe to the open end of the elbow on the lamp assembly. Pull the wires through the side opening of the T.

25. Use a pair of scissors to cut off the female end of a fabric-covered extension cord. You can easily make a cord for the lamp by connecting a male plug to the lamp cord included in the lamp-making kit, but

these fabric-covered extension cords are just too charming not to use.

26. Slide the compression adapter fitting over the cut cord, small end first. If your compression adapter is brass, and it probably is, give it a shot of flat silver spray paint before you do this step.

27. Insert the fabric cord into the bottom of the T fitting on the lamp neck and out of the side hole with the lamp cords. Twist the compression adapter into the hole on the bottom of the T.

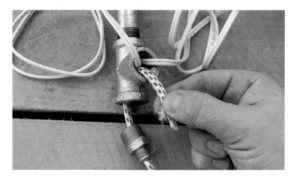

28. Use a pair of scissors to cut back the fabric covering on the extension cord and split the inner wires in half. Cut back the rubber coating and expose about 1½ inches of copper wire on each side.

29. Cut back the excess lamp cords and expose the copper wire on each of these as well.

30. Twist the lamp cords together. Right side to right side and left side to left side.

31. Gently twist the lamp cords together with the cut extension cord wires. Use wire nuts to tightly cover the connections. You can also secure this connection with electrical tape.

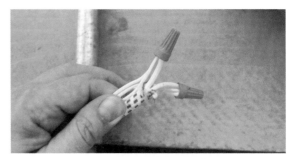

32. Attach a close nipple to the center of a T fitting and a plug to one of the open ends.

33. Gently push the lamp wires into the close nipple and attach the piece to the other T fitting to cover all the exposed wiring.

Remove the red handle from the gate valve with a pair of pliers and spritz the brass fixture with a flat silver spray paint. Allow to dry.

34. Combine the gate valve with a 2½-inch-long nipple and a 5-inch-long pipe. If your gate valve is brass, remove the knob with pliers and spray the base with a flat silver spray paint first.

35. Connect this piece to the underside of the T fitting.

36. Twist on the leg assembly to the bottom of the 5-inch-long pipe.

37. Attach the red knob back to the gate valve. This piece is purely decorative.

38. Screw the lightbulbs into the sockets and plug her in.

Perfect between two twin beds. Just like summer camp.

INDUSTRIAL NAPKIN RINGS

There's nothing stuffy about a dinner party at my house. Cocktails are served in Mason jars (if a guest breaks one, it's no loss), my dishes are mostly rescued from the chipped section of junk stores (the more "loved" they were, the more personality I think they have), and my napkins are usually kitchen towels.

What better "UN-stuffy" napkin rings than the steel octagon nut from a pipe union?

SUPPLIES

- 4 1-inch black iron joint pipe unions
- Napkins

TOOLS

- Orange industrial hand cleaner
- Cotton washcloth

Skill Level: **Easy**

Time: **5 minutes**

DIRECTIONS:

1. Pipe unions are designed so that two pipes can be disconnected in the future without disrupting the rest of the line. There are two types of unions: joint unions and flange unions. The easiest way to tell them apart is that joint unions have three parts and flange unions have two.

2. Unscrew the joint union.

3. Remove the inner nut and save the remaining pieces for another project.

4. Because unions are well-oiled and you don't want any of that oil staining your fine linens, it's important to wash them in orange industrial hand cleaner and warm water. Be sure to dry them thoroughly or they could rust.

Now your steel nuts are safe to slide over your fine linen napkins. Or kitchen towels—whichever you choose.

BIG RED HOOK

Sometimes you just need a place to hang your hat...or your robe... or a wet towel...or a dog leash. This big red hook is just that place.

SUPPLIES

- $^{15}/_{16}$-inch grade 43 clevis grab hook
- Glossy red spray paint
- ½ to ¼-inch compression adapter
- ½-inch flange
- 2½-inch machine screw with nut (size #10-32)
- Washer
- Flat metallic soft iron spray paint
- Self-drilling drywall anchors with screws

TOOLS

- Needle-nose pliers
- Cordless drill with screw-bit attachment
- Screwdriver
- Pencil

Skill Level: **Easy**

Time: **30 minutes, including dry time**

DIRECTIONS:

1. Clevis refers to the unthreaded pin at the top of the hook. With the needle-nose pliers, remove both of the pins from the hook. You won't need these so you can toss them.

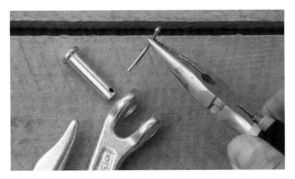

2. In a well-ventilated area, spray the hook a glossy red with a good-quality spray paint. Allow it to completely dry.

3. Tightly insert the compression adapter into the hole on top of the flange.

4. Paint the flange unit, and the machine screw and washer, with a spritz of flat metallic soft iron spray paint and allow to dry.

5. Slip the washer onto the machine screw. Insert the screw into the hole on the top of the clevis hook and through the hole in the top of the compression adapter.

6. Turn the flange over and twist on the nut that came with the machine screw with a pair of needle-nose pliers as tightly as it will go.

7. The best way to hang your finished hook is with self-drilling drywall anchors. They're available in plastic, but the best ones are galvanized because they also work in wood if you're lucky enough to hit a wall stud.

8. The screws that are included with the drywall anchors are unfortunately silver, and we want them to disappear on the newly painted flange. Just push them into the top of a cardboard box and spritz them with the same spray paint as the flange.

9. Anchoring just two screws in the wall are sufficient to hold the hook, there's no need to anchor all four screws. Mark the holes where you want to hang your hook on the wall with a pencil. Use the cordless drill to screw the anchors into the marks until they are flush with the wall.

10. Position the flange over the anchors holes and screw in the screws. Use a screwdriver so you don't scrape off any of the paint.

DOOR HANDLES

I'm not a fan of big box stores. I know, everybody has to shop there, but I like my home to have a little more individuality. Who wants a place that looks exactly like everyone else's? Not this guy.

When we found a small garden shed in a catalog, it was exactly the kind of outside storage we needed. But it was so plain. We enhanced it with a tin roof, cedar paneling, and a stain that matched our fence. But there was still something missing.

Handles. But not the kind of handles that anyone could find in any ol' store. We wanted something unique. Something exactly like these industrial pipe handles.

SUPPLIES

Use galvanized pipe and fittings.

- ¼ x 6-inch pipe
- 2 (¼-inch) street elbows
- 2 (½ to ¼-inch) reducing couplings
- 2 (½-inch) close nipples
- 2 (½-inch) flanges
- Spray paint
- ½-inch black screws

TOOLS

- Cordless drill with screw bit

Skill Level: **Easy**

Time: **About 15 minutes, plus dry time**

DIRECTIONS:

1. Lay out all your pieces. Note: Quarter-inch pipe and fittings may not be available in very many options at your local hardware store. Flanges can be hard-to-find fittings. The reducing couplings will fix this problem nicely.

2. Attach the 6-inch-long pipe to the 2 street elbows.

3. Be sure that the ends of both elbows are pointed in the same direction.

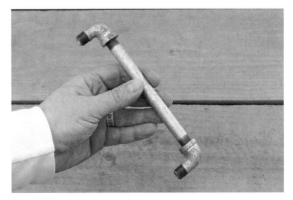

4. Attach the reducing couplings to the bottom half of the elbows.

5. Twist the close nipples into the flanges.

6. Attach the flange pieces to the bottoms of the couplings.

7. Make sure that both flanges are attached at an equal distance so your handle will lie flat against the door surface. You may think that the close nipple should disappear entirely into the other two pieces, but it won't. Some of the threads showing should be expected.

8. Spray the handles with spray paint in a well-ventilated area. I chose glossy black.

9. Use a cordless drill and the screws to attach the handles to the doors.

TIP: Any time you're going to use pipes outside, they need to be galvanized so they won't rust. Just use a good-quality spray paint to make them any color you'd like after they're assembled.

BIG PIPE BOOKENDS

My friend Lenny always says that books are "so decorative." But I have to disagree. I think they're more like trophies. I display them on shelves so that other people can take note of all of my accomplishments. Have I read every Armistead Maupin book? You better believe that I have. They're all lined up in a neat little row. In fact, every book I've ever read is on a shelf on our house somewhere. Here's the perfect way for you to feature a few of your favorite books.

SUPPLIES

Use 1-inch-diameter black pipe.

- 4 (1-inch) flanges
- 1 x 4-inch nipple
- 1 x 3-inch nipple
- 2 (90-degree) elbows
- 2 (1-inch) close nipples

TOOLS

Just your hands

Skill Level: **Easy**

Time: **5 minutes**

DIRECTIONS:

1. Start with the flanges. Add a 4-inch-long nipple to one and a 3-inch-long nipple to the other. You could make both bookends the same height, but I thought they were a little more interesting this way.

2. Twist a 90-degree elbow to the top of each nipple.

3. Add the close nipples to each open end of the elbows. Any connection bigger than these may make your bookends top heavy.

4. Finish off the assembly with the second set of flanges.

TABLETOP PIPE EASEL

There was a time when I wanted to be an animator for Walt Disney. Honestly, I was going to draw cartoons for a living. So my mother enrolled me in art classes at our community center. Every Saturday morning, I learned about form and fluidity, perspective, figure drawing, and color theory. But it was all just so much more tedious than I was expecting. When the class director scolded me in front of everyone for my terrible painting of a sun with a smiley face, I thought maybe this wasn't the class for me. After all, I wanted to be a cartoonist... and I was only 7 years old. Still, my mother cherished all those terrible smiley-face sun paintings that I brought home. If only she'd had this industrial tabletop easel to display them.

SUPPLIES:

Use ½-inch-diameter galvanized pipe and fittings.

- 4 street elbows
- 3 T fittings

- 4 square plugs
- 2 (5-inch) pipes
- 2 (2-inch) pipes
- 2 elbows

- 3 caps
- Cross fitting
- 3 close nipples
- 18-inch pipe

Skill Level: **Intermediate**

Time: **1 hour**

TOOLS

Just your hands

DIRECTIONS:

1. Start by adding a street elbow to each side of two of the T fittings.

2. Twist a square plug into the downward-facing hole of each street elbow to make the feet.

3. Thread each of the 5-inch-long pipes into the remaining holes on the two T fitting pieces.

4. Attach each of these pieces to the side openings of another T fitting to make the base of the easel. Give the hole in the T fitting a slight angle so the easel will pitch backward just a little.

5. Add a 2-inch-long pipe to each of the remaining elbows.

6. Finish each of these pipes with a cap.

7. Thread a close nipple into two corresponding sides of the cross fitting.

8. Attach the elbow pieces to the sides of the cross to make the arms of the easel.

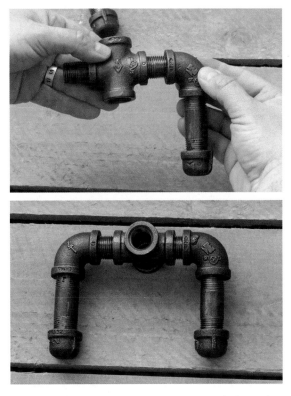

9. Thread the remaining close nipple into the top of the base assembly.

10. Attach the arms to the base of the easel.

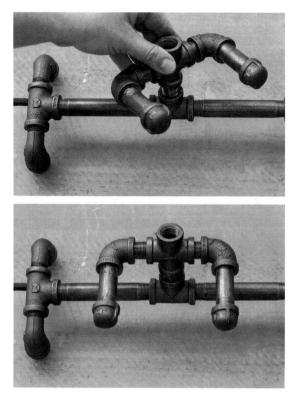

11. Attach the remaining cap to one end of the 18-inch-long pipe.

12. Screw the pipe into the top of the cross fitting on the arms to make the spine of the easel and you're done.

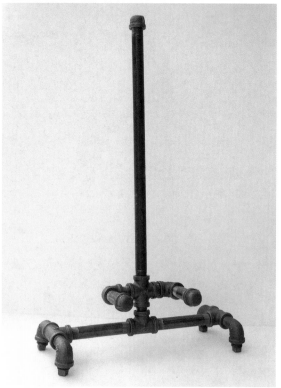

TABLETOP BOOK HOLDER

My love of books is entirely my mother's fault.

On family road trips my young mother would crawl into the backseat with my little brothers and I and read to us. Greek mythology, tales of King Arthur and his Knights of the Round Table, and *The Mad Scientists' Club* were all our favorites. But my absolute favorite stories were the Hardy Boys mysteries. Hands down. I loved how they were just average young men who were constantly stumbling into extraordinary mysteries.

When I discovered a handful of well-loved Hardy Boys books at a thrift store, I knew that I wasn't leaving without them. And I didn't. What better tribute for my favorite books than a custom pipe book holder?

SUPPLIES

Use ½-inch-diameter silver pipes and fittings.

- 2 cross fittings
- 4 (2½-inch) nipples
- 2 (2-inch) nipples
- 2 close nipples
- 4 elbow fittings
- 4 caps
- 2 (12-inch) pipes
- Felt pads

Skill Level: **Intermediate**　　　Time: **30 minutes**

TOOLS

Just your hands

DIRECTIONS:

1. Start with the cross fitting to make one side of the book holder. Add a 2½-inch-long nipple to one side of the cross. Working clockwise, add a 2½-inch-long nipple to the next side, a close nipple to the next side, and a 2-inch-long nipple on the last side.

Top one of the 2½-inch-long nipples with an elbow. Top the close nipple with an elbow. These will connect to the other side. Add a cap fitting to each of the remaining ends. These will be the feet.

2. Twist everything as tightly as it will go.

3. Repeat Step 1 on the other cross. But this time, turn the elbows until they face the opposite way of the first one. Match up the two sides to be sure that the end pieces mirror each other.

4. Each elbow will have a 12-inch-long pipe extending from it. Screw these in as far as they will go on one of the side pieces. But be careful not to make the connection too tight, because they will need to unscrew slightly to connect to the second side.

5. Line the pipes up with their corresponding elbows on the opposite side. As you twist the pipes into the unconnected elbows, they will slightly unscrew from the connected side. This may take a little work, twisting each side back and forth, but eventually the pipes will be connected to all four elbows.

6. Add felt pads to the bottoms of the feet to keep your book rack from scratching furniture, and you're done.

Mine is just the right size to hold 5-inch deep Hardy Boys books. You can customize the depth with the size of the nipples connecting the elbows to the cross. Simply add longer nipples to accommodate bigger books.

OCCASIONAL TABLE

When we moved into our house there was nothing in the backyard but a medium-sized square of concrete that I suppose was considered a *decent* patio in 1972. Now, not so much. We covered over that pathetic square with a 30 x 15-feet wooden deck. One side of the deck has steps that lead down to a layer of lush, green sod. We hung a few strings of cafe lights, and there's a fire pit now, surrounded by red Adirondack chairs, for roasting marshmallows all year long. Jamie found an outdoor sectional, and I covered it in bright serape pillows that we just sink into.

Now, we like to hang out in our back-yard. Sometimes there are 30 friends, sometimes it's just the two of us and our dog, Harley. Doesn't matter. Just as long as there's a place to set my beer. This little occasional table is just that place.

SUPPLIES

Use ¾-inch-diameter galvanized pipe and fittings.

- 15-inch round wood tabletop
- 18-inch round wood tabletop
- Turquoise wood stain
- 6 flanges
- ¾-inch silver screws
- 3 (18-inch) pipes

TOOLS

- Rubber gloves
- Cotton rag
- Tape measure
- Cordless drill with screw bit

Skill Level: **Easy**   Time: **½ hour, plus dry time**

DIRECTIONS:

1. Wearing rubber gloves, stain the tabletops with the turquoise stain. Wipe it on both sides with a clean cotton rag, covering every inch, and allow to dry completely. It doesn't have to be turquoise. Choose any color you like. I just thought a bright, sunny color would be fun on the deck.

2. Position three of the flanges near the middle of the smaller wood top for the table base.

3. Make sure they are just about 2 inches apart.

4. With a cordless drill, attach the flanges with ¾-inch silver screws.

5. Screw an 18-inch-long pipe into each flange.

6. Add the remaining flanges to the tops of each pipe tightly. With a tape measure, make sure the height of each is the same: about 18¾ inches.

7. Flip the base unit over and onto the bottom of the second, larger tabletop.

8. Position the flanges so that they are in the middle of this wood top also. They don't have to be perfect, but each should be about 4 inches from the edge.

9. Using your cordless drill, screw these flanges on with silver screws.

10. Flip your table over so that the smaller disk becomes the bottom.

ANGLE-LEGGED CONSOLE

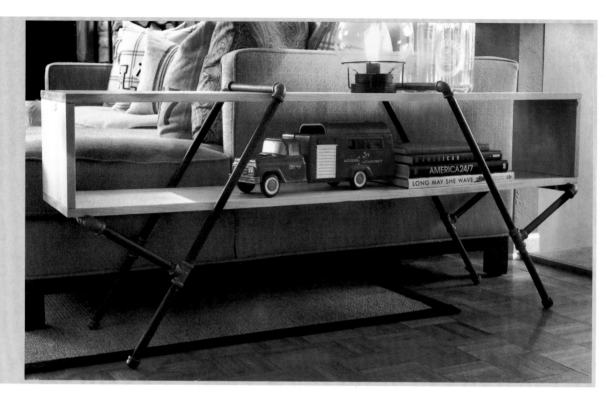

I've seen a lot of industrial pipe furniture on the Web. But there aren't many that blend modern with industrial as much as this console does. When we couldn't seem to find just the right furniture piece to hug the edge of our sofa, I built this console in the perfect dimensions to fit my space.

Try it for yourself. You can easily modify this design to fit your own home. If the box is too long, make it smaller. If the height is too tall, shorten the legs. Or, make one exactly like mine following these simple instructions.

SUPPLIES

Use ½-inch-diameter black pipes and fittings.

- 8 elbows
- 8 (12-inch) pipes
- 4 (18-inch) pipes

- 4 T fittings
- 4 (8-inch) pipes
- 4 caps
- 2 (1 x 12 x 60-inch) pine boards

- 2 (1 x 12 x 11-inch) pine boards
- Wood stain in your choice of color
- 4 U-shaped straps
- ½-inch screws

TOOLS

- Tape measure
- Clean rag
- Rubber gloves
- Wood glue
- Brad gun
- 2 large wood clamps
- Cordless drill with screw bit

Skill Level: **Intermediate**   Time: **Just over an hour**

DIRECTIONS: **FOR THE PIPE LEG BASE**

1. Attach an elbow fitting to each end of a 12-inch-long pipe.

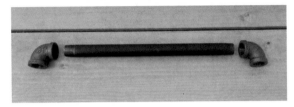

2. Using a tape measure, be sure the distance between the fittings is smaller than the width of the wood for the box. Usually a "12-inch-wide board" is *really* about 11¼ inches wide because of wood shrinkage. My distance is just slightly bigger than 11¼ inches. Perfect.

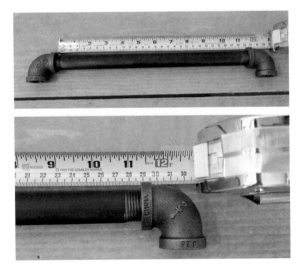

3. Attach the two 18-inch-long pipes to the bottoms of the elbow fittings. This will be the sides of the frame for the legs.

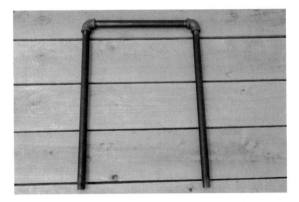

4. Add a T fitting to the bottom of these two 18-inch-long pipes.

5. Aim the side opening for each T fitting straight up so they can hold the brace piece.

6. Use a tape measure to check the distance of the T fitting on each side of the leg fixture. The exact distance doesn't matter, just that they line up equally. In this case, both of mine measure 19½ inches.

7. Use another 12-inch-long pipe, two elbows, and two 8-inch-long pipes to create the "brace" in our leg piece. Again, making sure the distance between the two elbows is

slightly larger than 11¼ inches to accommodate the size of the box.

8. Push the brace piece down into the two T side openings completed in Step 7 and screw the 8-inch-long pipes in. You will be unscrewing them from the elbows a little in order to re-screw them into the T's on the leg piece. This can take a little work to get good connections all around, but I promise, it will happen.

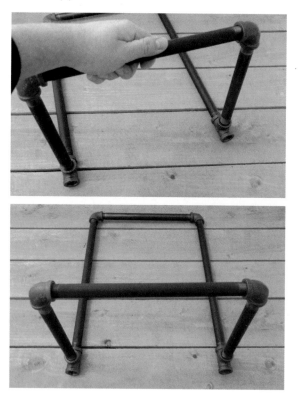

9. Attach a cap to the end of two 12-inch-long pipes. These will be the console's feet.

10. These screw into the bottom hole of the T fitting on the base piece.

11. Repeat steps 1–11 to create a second pipe leg base. You will need two bases in order for the unit to stand correctly.

DIRECTIONS: **FOR THE BOX**

1. With a clean rag and rubber gloves to protect your hands, stain the wood on all sides in your choice of stain (I used a water-based "honey" color), and allow to dry according to the directions on the can.

2. To connect the boards, add a line of wood glue to the edge of the smaller interior 11-inch board.

TIP: Most home improvement stores will cut wood for you to size. Just ask.

3. With the 60-inch boards on the top and bottom, use a brad gun to nail the sides together. (You could use nails, but a brad gun is actually much easier and makes smaller holes.)

DIRECTIONS: **FOR THE CONSOLE**

1. Lay the two leg pieces back to back, at a slight angle.

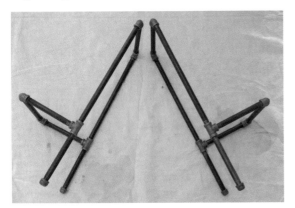

4. Clamp the box together with large clamps and allow the wood glue to dry overnight.

2. Slowly insert the box from the side. Be careful not to drag the wood across the black metal pipes or it may rub off on the light-colored wood.

3. Position the leg pieces so that the bottom brace of each is at the very end of the bottom of each side of the box. Push the feet outward so that the top of each leg brace is resting on the top of the box. Like so.

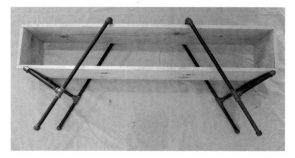

4. Gravity alone will make your console stand up, but it's probably a good idea to attach a few U-straps anyway.

5. On the underside of the wood box, where nobody will see them, use a cordless drill and ½-inch screws to attach the pipe legs to the wood box with the U-straps.

6. Turn the console over so that it rests on its feet and enjoy your new modern/industrial console. This could be perfect in an entryway to store shoes, or even under a wall-mounted TV.

INDUSTRIAL DOG BED

The picture of her made me smile. Her personality just beamed through my monitor. She was standing on someone's bed (one of my biggest pet peeves about dogs), with a big foam ball in her mouth. Her head was cocked, her good ear straight up in the air and the other flopping down, and she was looking right at the camera. I knew it was because the photographer had just called her name: Harley Davidson. Such a perfect name.

She was only a 20-minute drive from our house, and we made arrangements to "just meet" her that afternoon. We knew in that instant she was the one.

We brought Harley Davidson home with us, and we made her this industrial dog bed. So she would have a *forever* home, and a bed of her own.

SUPPLIES

Use black pipes and fittings.

- 2 (2 x 6 x 39-inch) wood boards, mitered at 45 degrees
- 2 (2 x 6 x 27-inch) wood boards, mitered at 45 degrees
- Wood stain in brown
- 3-inch lag screws
- 4 (4-inch) corner brackets with screws
- 8 (½-inch) flanges
- 1-inch drywall screws
- 4 (½ x 3-inch) pipes
- 3-inch round self-adhesive felt pads
- 4 (½ to ⅜-inch) reducing elbows
- 2 (½ x 18-inch) pipes
- 4 (⅜ x 2½-inch) pipes
- ¾ x 35½ x 23½-inch plywood sheet
- 4-inch-thick foam pad (cut 36 inches by 24 inches)
- Mexican serape blanket

TOOLS

- Sand paper
- Chain, hammer, small crowbar
- Cotton rag
- Rubber gloves
- Cordless drill with screw bit
- ¼-inch drill bit
- Hex socket bit
- ⅝-inch paddle bit
- Rubber mallet

Skill Level: **Intermediate**   Time: **About 2 hours**

DIRECTIONS:

1. For a reclaimed wood look, beat the four 2 x 6 sides with a chain, hammer, small crowbar, anything that will mar the surface. I find the chain works best. There isn't possibly a wrong way to do this, so really take some frustrations out on the wood. Be as random as you can with the marks and careful not to crush the mitered edges.

See the difference that "damaging" the wood a little can make?

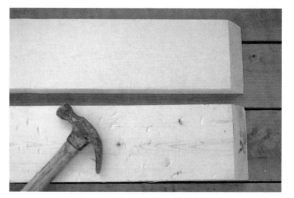

2. Stain the wood pieces with your choice of stain. I used a dark, rich Minwax Jacobean. Simply wipe it on with a clean cotton cloth. Be sure to protect your hands with rubber gloves. The dark stain will settle into the grooves and rough spots, making them even more visible. This is exactly what you want it to do.

3. After the stain has completely dried, drill pilot holes into the sides of the 2 x 6s for the lag screws with a ¼-inch drill bit. The front and back boards get two holes on each end, close to the top and bottom. The side boards get one hole at each end, directly in the middle.

TIP: To miter or not to miter? Cutting the boards at a 45-degree angle is called "mitering" and requires a little more time and patience. It's not necessary, but your finished dog bed will look much more professional if you do. So give it a try. If you decide to do flat edges, change the length of the smaller boards from 27 inches long to 24 inches.

4. With a hex socket bit attached to the cordless drill, screw in the lag screws to connect all four sides of the box. When you connect the four sides, the lag screws will overlap each other. Your wood seams at the corners don't need to be perfect. In fact, *slightly* imperfect will only enhance the rustic character of the bed.

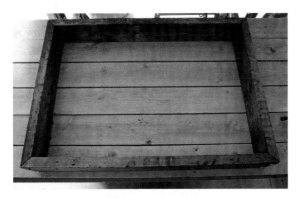

5. Attach the corner braces to the inside of the box with the 1-inch screws included in the pack. These should be as close to the bottom as they will go. Of course they hold the bottom of the bed in place, but they'll also help strengthen the box.

6. Add a flange in each corner of the underside of the box for the feet. Adjust the flange so that three of the holes line up with wood, and attach with drywall screws.

7. Twist a 3-inch-long pipe into each flange.

8. Top each 3-inch-long pipe with another flange.

9. Cover each of these flanges with a 3-inch-round self-adhesive felt pad to keep the bed from scratching your floors. If you don't have hardwood floors, you can probably skip the pads.

10. To make the side rails, add a reducing elbow to each end of the 18-inch-long pipes.

11. To the open end of the elbows, twist on the 2½-inch-long pipes.

12. Place the rails where you think they need to be in the center of the sides of the box, and give each end a good whack with a rubber mallet. Don't be gentle. It will leave a little round mark from the pipe.

13. With a cordless drill fitted with a ⅝-inch paddle bit, drill out a hole about an inch deep.

14. Place the railing back over the freshly drilled holes and give it a couple good pounds with a rubber mallet to drive the pipes into the holes. These aren't really handles, they are more of just a decorative railing.

15. Place the plywood bottom into the finished box resting on the corner brackets. There's really no need to stain it, unless you're a perfectionist, because it won't be seen.

16. Any blanket will work, but I prefer the look of Mexican serape blankets. Wrap the blanket around the foam piece, folding the edges just like you would wrap a present. Hopefully you will want to wash this occasionally so just secure the ends with a few big safety pins so it can be removed easily.

17. Slip the blanket-covered foam into the finished dog bed and prepare yourself for a happy best friend.

I realize that this is a pretty big dog bed, and not everyone has a moose of a dog like Harley Davidson. (She's about 80 pounds.) You can easily adjust the dimensions of the bed to fit your size of dog. Or simply adopt a bigger dog like we did.

ROLLING SIDE TABLE

This is a pretty basic project, but extremely versatile. Mine is currently in the guest room as a nightstand but I added the casters so we could roll it from room to room whenever we need an extra cocktail table. (Which is more often than we'd like to publicly admit.) Once you get the concept down, this table can be modified to be bigger for a dining table or shorter for a coffee table. Your choice.

SUPPLIES

Use ½-inch-diameter black pipes and fittings.

- 24-inch round wood tabletop
- Number stencils
- Brown stain

- Darker brown stain
- 4 (4-inch) casters
- 4 (8-inch) pipes
- 4 (6-inch) pipes
- 4 (x 18-inch) pipes
- Flat black spray paint

- Cross fitting
- 4 T fittings
- Rubber tubing
- 4 flanges
- ¾-inch screws

TOOLS

- Painter's tape
- Pencil
- Wood burner

- Rubber gloves
- Cotton rag
- Small paintbrush

- Screwdriver
- Rubber mallet

- Drill with screw bit attachment

Skill Level: **Intermediate**   Time: **1 hour, plus dry time**

DIRECTIONS: **FOR THE TABLETOP**

I could have left the top plain, but decided to jazz it up a bit with our house number. But I could have easily gone with a monogram or even initials. If you've never used a wood burner before, give it a try. It's the perfect way to add some personality to a wood piece.

1. Lay the stencils in place and tape them down so they don't slide.

2. Trace the inside of the numbers with a pencil and peel off the stencils.

3. Use the wood burner to "draw" along the pencil lines of your numbers.

4. Go slow and steady. The harder you push down, the deeper the burn will be. (It's not a bad idea to try this on a scrap piece of wood before tackling your tabletop.)

5. Stain the tabletop using wood stain in your choice of color. (I used Minwax Jacobean.) Wear rubber gloves to keep your hands clean, and simply wipe on the stain in the direction of the wood grain with a cotton rag.

6. After the stain is completely dry according to the dry time on the can, use a small paintbrush to add a slightly darker stain to the inside of the burned numbers.

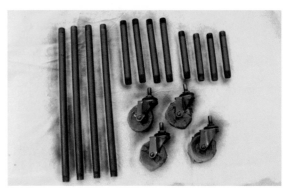

DIRECTIONS: **FOR THE BASE**

1. Tape off the wheels of the casters with painter's tape.

2. Give all the pipes and the casters a coating of flat black spray paint.

3. Start with the cross fitting. Add all four 8-inch-long pipes to the cross fitting and screw until tight.

4. Then, twist on the T fitting to the end of each pipe. Aimed up.

5. Now add a 6-inch-long pipe to the end of each T; these will be the bottom half of each leg.

6. To keep the casters tight inside the pipe, cut a piece of rubber tubing about 1½ inches long.

7. Slip the rubber tubing over the screw end of the caster.

8. Use a screwdriver and the rubber mallet to "bang" the casters into each leg pipe. It will (and should) be a tight fit.

9. Flip it over onto the wheels.

10. Screw the 18-inch-long pipes into the open end of each T fitting to extend the leg upward.

11. Top each one with a flange.

12. Use the ¾-inch screws to attach the table base to the underside of the tabletop.

13. Flip it over, and enjoy your new side table. The finished table should be somewhere between 28 and 30 inches tall.

LOCKER BASKET DRESSER

In my childhood summers, my mother would take my brothers and me swimming at the public pool. It wasn't the most glamorous of places, but it wasn't without certain charms either. Of course it was fun to slide down the waterslide and see which of us could hold his breath underwater the longest. But my favorite part didn't have anything to do with the water at all. I was fascinated with the enormous wall of metal locker baskets outside the changing rooms that we used to keep our "street clothes" in. Although each basket drawer was only about a foot square, we just needed one to store all three boy's T-shirts, shorts, and flip-flops while we swam.

I've been collecting these old locker baskets for years because they just remind me of those long summers. Every time I found one in a junk shop, I'd buy it, regardless of the condition. The more worn-in it was, the more stories I'm sure it had to tell. When I finally had a dozen, a nice even number, I thought that maybe I should do *something* with them—like recreate that wall of swim baskets I remember so fondly from the public pool.

Only *slightly* smaller. Let's call it a dresser.

SUPPLIES

Use ½-inch galvanized pipe and fittings.

- 4 (1 x 14 x 56-inch) Aspen wood shelves
- Gray stain
- 6 (7-inch) pipes
- 12 unions
- 12 flanges
- ½-inch silver screws
- 6 (8-inch) pipes
- 6 (9-inch) pipes
- 2 x 12 x 54-inch board
- 16 (1-inch) silver lag screws
- 4 silver swivel casters
- 2-inch silver screws
- 12 vintage metal locker baskets
- 12 silver eye hooks
- Combination locks

TOOLS

- Clean cotton rag
- Rubber gloves
- Tape measure
- Pencil
- Cordless drill with screw bit
- Hex socket bit
- ⅞-inch paddle bit
- Wood clamps
- 2 x 4s, for leverage

Skill Level: **Intermediate**   Time: **About 2 hours, plus dry time**

DIRECTIONS:

My baskets are just about 13 inches deep, so my wood shelves need to be slightly larger at 14 inches.

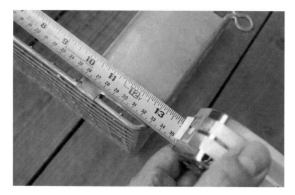

TIP: Don't have the time to search every antique mall in your area for a dozen of these old locker baskets? Try looking online on eBay, Etsy, and Craigslist. There are plenty to be had. Expect to pay anywhere from $15 to $30 for each, plus shipping. New baskets, similar to the old-school version, can be found at the Container Store, Target, and even Crate & Barrel.

1. Use precut Aspen wood panels from the hardware store. They are a perfect choice for furniture building. Aspen is soft enough to cut and drill into easily, it's not too heavy and, best of all, it stains very nicely. Stain the wood shelves, top, bottom, and sides, in a water-based gray stain. Use a clean cotton rag and be sure to wear gloves to protect your hands.

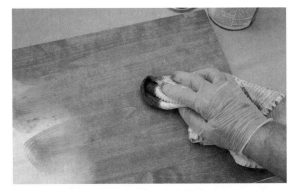

2. Because flanges come in slightly different sizes, determine where they are going to land on the bottom shelf. They should be just next to the edges of the wood.

3. Mark the distance for six pipe holes at the corners and center of the shelf with a pencil. The center point for each flange should be 1¾ inches from each side of the shelf, and from the center edge.

4. Use a few clamps to clamp the two center shelves tightly together, and elevate them on 2 x 4s so the paddle bit will pierce all the way though both shelves without damaging the work surface underneath.

5. You will need to use a paddle bit for drilling all six holes for the support pipes in the two center shelves. To accommodate a ½-inch pipe, you will need to use a ⅞-inch paddle bit for the holes. (Remember, ½-inch refers to the inside diameter of the pipe, not the outside.)

6. Using a cordless drill with the ⅞-inch paddle bit attachment, drill holes for the support pipes all the way through both center shelf boards at the same time. Be sure to push the drill straight down and not at an angle.

7. As an extra precaution to keep the shelves from sliding apart while you're drilling, insert a loose pipe into each freshly drilled hole.

8. It's crucial to keep your holes in both shelves perfectly in line with each other.

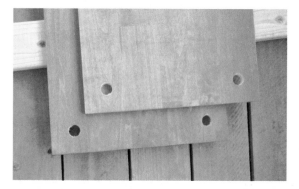

9. Wipe some stain around the freshly drilled holes to hide any damages the paddle bit may have caused. Set these two shelves aside to dry.

10. Start building the shelf unit with the six 7-inch-long pipes. Attach a flange at one end and a union at the other. Tighten them until they are all slightly over 8 inches tall. Since the baskets are 8 inches tall, you'll want the distance between shelves to be just large enough to fit the basket. These will be the first layer of the support pipes on the bottom shelf.

11. With a cordless drill and ½-inch screws, screw the flanges to the bottom shelf. Remember to be sure to position the center of the pipe 1¾ inches from the edges to line up with the holes of the next shelf.

12. When all six supports are attached, lay one of the middle shelves on top and line up the holes with each corresponding union underneath.

13. Insert the 8-inch-long pipes next, one in each hole, and gently screw into the union below.

14. Top each of these pipes with a union as well, and carefully measure so that each pipe is just about 8 inches high. All three shelves don't have to be the exact same distance apart, just enough so that the locker baskets will slide under them loosely.

15. Top this row with the next shelf. Again, line up the holes with the unions beneath. Screw the remaining 9-inch-long pipes into these.

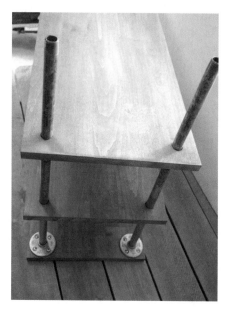

16. Top the final pipes with the remaining six flanges. Measure to make sure they are all about the same height.

17. Lay the final shelf on top and attach the flanges from underneath with ½-inch screws.

18. Stain the edges of the 2 x 12 with gray stain. There's no need to stain the top and bottom because no one will ever see them. Think of it as a kind of skateboard for the shelves to roll on.

19. Once the stain is dry, attach the casters to the bottom of the board with the lag screws. Lag screws require a hex socket bit, and are a much tighter connection to the board than regular screws.

20. Flip over the shelving unit and lay the caster piece on the underside, leaving about an inch of shelf around all four sides.

21. Attach the caster piece to the bottom of the shelf unit with a few 2-inch screws.

22. Flip the unit over onto the wheels and insert the locker baskets into the shelves.

23. Use a drill with a small drill bit to drill a pilot hole centered over each basket.

24. Twist an eye hook into each pilot hole to correspond with the loop on the basket below.

25. Not that I'm still worried about someone stealing my clothes, but just for fun, I added a few old-school combination locks. (Be sure to leave the combinations taped to the back if you plan on locking them.)

WALL-MOUNTED BOOKSHELVES

I can't remember a time when I didn't have any books. Seriously, they've been a joy and a burden all my life. I only say "burden" because I've had to move all of them a few times. And the good Lord knows that I would never part with a book. With bookshelves like these, you'll never have to either.

SUPPLIES

Use ¾-inch-diameter black pipe and fittings.

- 4 (4-inch) nipples
- 20 flanges
- 24 T fittings
- 12 (8-inch) pipes
- 12 (1-inch) nipples

- ½-inch black drywall screws
- 3 (1 x 12 x 120-inch) pine boards
- 12 (10-inch) pipes
- 1 x 4 x 120-inch pine board
- 4 (1 x 4 x 15-inch) pine board

- 1 x 14 x 120-inch pine board
- 1 x 2 x 120-inch pine board
- Finishing nails
- Steel wool
- Vinegar

TOOLS

- Tape measure
- Pencil
- Cordless drill with screw bit
- 1-inch paddle bit

- Scrap 2 x 4s
- Heavy grit sandpaper
- Hand saw
- Small chisel

- Hammer
- Level
- Nail gun
- Paintbrush

Skill Level: **Advanced**   Time: **A few hours**

DIRECTIONS:

1. Make the four footings for the shelves by connecting each of the four 4-inch-long nipples to a flange.

2. To make the arms for holding the first shelf, attach each footing piece from step #1 to the bottom hole of a T fitting. Then continue the arm assembly with an 8-inch-long pipe, a second T fitting, a 1-inch-long nipple, and a flange. Be sure that the side opening on the T fitting is aimed upward.

3. There's not a standard height for the bottom shelf, but it is important that all four footings are the same distance from the floor. In this case, 5¾-inches from the top of the flange to the top of the T fitting.

4. Distance the four footings 30 inches apart from each other and attach the flange on the back of the arm assembly to the wall with drywall screws. You can also screw your flange into the floor for added support, but it isn't really necessary. Your shelves will be plenty sturdy if you don't.

5. Mark out the locations for the pipe holes in the three 1 x 12 shelves. The four pipes should be about 30 inches apart and 15 inches from each side. Mark each distance 1-inch from the edge of the shelves.

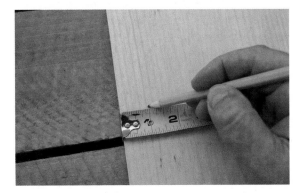

6. Choose a paddle bit that is slightly larger than the diameter of your pipe. Remember that ¾-inch pipe refers to the inside dimension of the pipe so a 1-inch paddle will work just fine.

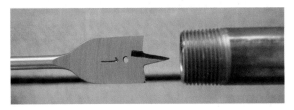

7. Use scrap 2 x 4s to prop the shelves off the work surface. Push the drill straight down to make your holes in the three shelf boards. Use sandpaper to finish any rough edges around the holes.

8. Lay the wood shelf across the shelf brackets and insert a 10-inch-long pipe into each hole, connecting it to the T fitting below. The back of the shelf will rest on the upturned T fitting on the back of each pipe assembly just about 2 inches from the wall.

9. Continue adding the next two shelves, building eight more arm assemblies and attaching each to the wall with drywall screws. Use the tape measure to make sure the shelf brackets are all the same distance from each other so your shelves aren't wonky. Top the third row of 10-inch-long pipes with the remaining four flanges.

10. To make the cleat for the top of the bookshelves, use a pencil to mark the locations of the wood braces on the 10-foot 1 x 4. The brackets should lie at the same distances as the holes in each shelf for the pipe braces—30 inches apart and 15 inches from the ends of each board.

11. Use one of the 1 x 4 pine braces as a template by centering it over the pencil mark and tracing the board at the top edge of the cleat board.

12. Use a hand saw to cut straight down the side marks on the cleat board.

13. On a solid surface, tap the chisel with the hammer along the bottom pencil line. Pine is a soft wood and breaks off pretty easily.

14. Use a heavy grit sandpaper to smooth the cutout so the wood brace will lie flat in the groove.

15. With a level, make sure the cleat is level and attach it to the wall with drywall screws.

16. Each notch in the wall cleat should line up with a flange at the top of each pipe assembly.

17. The height of the cleat and the height of flanges at the tops of the pipe supports should be 42½ inches.

18. The distance from the wall to the edge of each flange should be just about 14½ inches.

19. Lay the four 1 x 4 x 15-inch wood braces into the openings on the cleat and onto the flange at the top of each pipe shelf support. There's no need to attach the wood braces to the cleat, but screw each flange to the underside of the wood brace with ½-inch drywall screws.

20. Lay the 1 x 14-inch board across the top of the wood brackets and attach it with a few finishing nails.

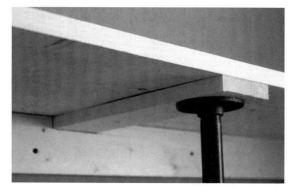

21. To hide the rough edge of the top, attach the 1 x 2 along the edge with small finishing nails.

22. Put the steel wool in a mason jar of vinegar and let it sit for a few days until the steel wool breaks down. It will look like a nasty mess, but something in the chemical makeup will age the wood. Just brush it on with a paintbrush.

23. Allow the vinegar mixture to dry completely, at least overnight, before covering your new shelves with books.

TIP: At this point you could stain your new shelves with the stain color of your choice, but I thought it would be a little more unique to "pickle" the wood with steel wool and vinegar.

RESOURCES

Pipes, pipe nipples, pipe fittings: Most traditional hardware stores will carry everything you need. Try HomeDepot.com, Lowes.com, Amazon.com, and AceHardware.com. There are also several online retailers worth checking out too: PlumbingFittingsDirect.com and SupplyHouse.com.

Cloth-covered extension cords: These are a must for a vintage industrial look. Find them at Amazon.com, Lowes.com, Etsy.com, and ConwayGoods.com. Or, buy the wire itself and add your own plug from SundialWire.com and SchoolhouseElectric.com.

Edison-style vintage lightbulbs: These are pretty popular right now. Find them at your local hardware store, HomeDepot.com, Lowes.com, Amazon.com, and AceHardware.com. Or you can buy them at specialty lightbulb stores: LightingSupply.com, or 1000Bulbs.com.

Lamp parts/kits: Stores that stock lamp parts exclusively are a good bet. Find them at SundialWire.com, AntiqueLampSupply.com, HomeDepot.com, and Lowes.com.

Vintage-style locker baskets: There are plenty of new baskets available at ContainerStore.com and CrateandBarrel.com. Or, search for the real vintage baskets at Etsy.com and Ebay.com.

Wire cages: These are easy to find at Amazon.com, 100Bulbs.com, and ShadesofLight.com.

Galvanized pots: Craft stores should have a few options. Try Ikea.com, HobbyLobby.com, Michaels.com, and JoAnn.com.

Casters: Pretty common at hardware stores like HarborFreight.com, HomeDepot.com, and Lowes.com. But there are also retailers that sell only casters, like Uline.com and CasterCity.com.

Serape blankets: If you aren't planning a trip to Mexico anytime soon, buy them online at Mexicanblankets.com, ElpasoSaddleBlanket.com, Etsy.com, and Amazon.com.

Orange hand cleaner: Find this at AutoZone.com, NapaOnline.com, Sears.com, Amazon.com, or HarborFreight.com.

ACKNOWLEDGMENTS

My mother says that when I was only five, she knew I wasn't like all the other little boys. So she encouraged me to take art classes, and to cook, and to garden. When I said that I didn't think I saw the world the same way that everyone else does, she told me that was a gift. When I said that I wanted to be a writer, she bought me a Casio typewriter. Twenty-eight years later, I finally wrote that book. She told me that she never doubted that I would. Thank you, Mom.

Thanks also go to Suella Clark and Ruthlynn Aalen, for seeing talents in a young me that I didn't yet know were there. Cathy Shields, Ivan Walton, and Tim Albrecht, where would my path have taken me if I hadn't met you three? My brothers, Josh and Ben, who answered all my annoying questions at annoying hours of the day. Sherry and John Petersnick, Daniel Kanter, and Karianne Wood, fellow (and much more successful than me) bloggers whose writing/photographing/designing skills continue to inspire me daily. Casie Vogel, for that initial tweet and for being my patient guide through this process. Martha, Walt, Jim, George, and Ralph, because passion and a belief in yourself can take you anywhere.

Lastly, and by far most importantly, I have to thank Jamie. (If you can see both my hands in a picture, Jamie took it. If you only see one of my hands, he did the editing.) Your constant belief in me has kept me going these past few months. You are my partner, my backbone, and my best friend. You're the most patient man I've ever known (I know that I push that limit sometimes), and I could not have done all this without you.

Well, I could have...but it would have taken much longer.

ABOUT THE AUTHOR

James Angus is a stylist/set designer currently living in Dallas, Texas, with his partner, Jamie, and their adopted Doberman, Harley Davidson. After a couple decades of working for retail giants like Saks Fifth Avenue, Louis Vuitton, and Ralph Lauren, he has experience as an artist, a floral designer, a photographer, an event planner; and now, after publishing his first book, a writer. For the past seven years, he has been documenting the renovation process of his Oak Cliff home on the moderately popular blog, *TheCavenderDiary*.com. With a design style he calls "Modern Industrial Western Flea Market," he is always looking for new ways to use industrial pipe around his house.